P9-DEB-518

Also by James Carville

HAD ENOUGH?

STICKIN': THE CASE FOR LOYALTY

. . . AND THE HORSE HE RODE IN ON

WE'RE RIGHT, THEY'RE WRONG

ALL'S FAIR *(with Mary Matalin)*

Also by Paul Begala

IT'S *STILL* THE ECONOMY, STUPID

"IS OUR CHILDREN LEARNING?": THE CASE AGAINST
GEORGE W. BUSH

James Carville

& Paul Begala

Simon & Schuster
New York London Toronto Sydney

Buck Up,
Suck Up...
and
Come Back
When
You
Foul Up

**12
WINNING
SECRETS
FROM THE
WAR
ROOM**

SIMON & SCHUSTER
Rockefeller Center
1230 Avenue of the Americas
New York, New York 10020

Copyright © 2002 by James Carville and Paul Begala
All rights reserved, including the right of reproduction
in whole or in part in any form.

First Simon & Schuster trade paperback edition 2003

"Paul Begala's Boys' French Toast" recipe from The Cook's Bible
by Christopher Kimball. © 1996 by Christopher Kimball. Reprinted
by permission of Little, Brown and Company, (Inc.)

SIMON & SCHUSTER and colophon are registered trademarks of Simon & Schuster Inc.

For information about special discounts for bulk purchases,
please contact Simon & Schuster Special Sales:
1-800-456-6798 or business@simonandschuster.com

Designed by Karolina Harris
Manufactured in the United States of America

10   9   8   7   6   5   4   3   2   1

The Library of Congress has cataloged the hardcover edition as follows:
Carville, James.
Buck up, suck up—and come back when you foul up : 12 winning secrets
from the war room.
p. cm.
Includes bibliographical references.
1. Success. 2. Conduct of life. 3. Political ethics. I. Begala, Paul. II Title.
BJ1611 .C366 2002
158—dc21   2002524021

ISBN 0-7432-2422-1
ISBN 0-7432-3448-0 (Pbk)

For John and Willie:
"Had we but world enough and time . . ."

Paul

For Miz Nippy, 1918–2001

James

Contents

Acknowledgments

So many people helped to make this book come about—
not the least of whom are the many political candidates
who gave us their trust and confidence over the years. We
learned from every one of them, and we hope their wisdom is adequately reflected here.

Paul would especially like to thank his mother and step-
father, Peggy and Jerry Howard, who loaned him their
computer and splashed in the pool with his kids so that he
could work on this project. Paul's in-laws, Jean and Dean
Friday, also contributed their laptop and their baby-sitting
services. Paul's dad, David Begala, offered sage advice and
sanity-saving fishing trips, and his sister, Kathleen, was his
consigliere, cheerleader and favorite sister.

Both James and Paul particularly want to recognize the
many contributions of Dalit Toledano, who painstakingly
researched, fact-checked and edited this little tome. Dalit
proved yet again that she is as talented as she is decent—
and she's the most decent person we know.

Dave McNeely of the *Austin American-Statesman* and
Beverly Reeves and Amy Todd of the Austin law firm of
Vinson and Elkins provided hard-to-find research on a
long-ago Texas scandal that provides a powerful lesson for

today. Keith Mason was a helpful resource on politics in general and Georgia in particular. Bob Barnett, aided by Kathleen Ryan, proved to be both an able attorney and a good friend. David Rosenthal and Geoff Kloske of Simon & Schuster had endless faith and a surprisingly deep reservoir of patience for this project, for which we're grateful. Those whom we contacted to assist in this book, from Tim Russert to Tom DeLay to Hillary Rodham Clinton, were unstinting in their generosity. James's old pal Gus Weill of Baton Rouge was a wealth of wisdom. And our dear friend Mark Weiner was and is a real winner.

Above all, Paul would like to thank Diane—for giving him all the things that matter in life, especially the four things that make it worth living: John, Billy, Charlie and Patrick. Paul would have dedicated this book to Diane, as he did his last one, but his whole life is dedicated to her anyway.

And James would like to thank Mary, Matty and Emma . . . for everything.

Buck Up,
Suck Up...
and
Come Back
When
You
Foul Up

Introduction

THIS book won't change your life.

If you buy this book and read it, you will not make $1 million—at least not because you bought this book. This ain't the New Testament or the Tibetan Book of the Dead or the Talmud or the Koran. Buying it won't cause the *Today* show to do a one-hour special on you, and the opposite sex (or the same sex if that's what floats your boat) will not suddenly find you irresistible.

Here's what you'll get: good, sound advice on how to win. You'll get techniques and tactics that are battle-tested and proven in the white-hot crucible of politics.

In writing this book, we've learned a lot. As intuitive, trust-your-gut political strategists, we're a far cry from the political philosophers or political scientists who have dissected political strategy in scholarly texts. Nor are we corporate turnaround artists, self-help gurus, motivational speakers, retired CEOs or former coaches. All of them have written books that offer unique insights into the game of life as played on their turf.

But our turf is different. American politics at the dawn of the twenty-first century is a brutal, bloody, winner-take-all game. As it should be. The stakes in political combat are not multibillion-dollar mergers or championship rings. Those things are nice, and we're sure they're important to the folks who have a stake in them. But America and the world will not long remember or care whether Ford or GM had the bestselling family minivan, much less whether the Lakers can "three-peat" or Tiger Woods shanks a drive.

There are no higher stakes than determining who runs the only superpower on God's earth. Politics matters. It determines in large measure whether the Dow Jones Industrial Average goes up or down. It determines whether unemployment goes up or down. Whether the welfare rate and the crime rate and the prime rate go up or down— whether America itself goes up or down. Politics, as John F. Kennedy Jr. used to say, is the only game for grown-ups— and too important to be left to the politicians.

And the best thing about American politics is that, on Election Day, you matter more than all the special-interest groups and all the pundits and all the corporations. Because with your vote you decide the fate and future of the greatest nation in human history. That's why, while we never take ourselves seriously, we always took our work in political campaigns very seriously. Candidates have entrusted us with their life's dream, with their fondest hopes, their deepest ambitions, their darkest secrets.

The two of us combined represent nearly a half-century of involvement in politics. From local judicial races to the presidency, we've won some, we've lost some and we've blown some. And along the way we've learned a lot. A Carville-Begala campagin had certain attributes, some of them accidental, but most of them intentional, that reflected our approach to our craft.

We believe our approach is different from most of what you'd find in corporate life for one very simple reason: in business a 49 percent market share means you're rich. In campaigns it means you're through. In our business there is only absolute victory and abject defeat—and both your victories and your defeats are played out on the front page of newspapers. That kind of zero-sum game, with those kinds of stakes, sharpens your approach.

Will political lessons translate to your corporate culture, your life, your work, your country? You'll have to judge for yourself. But we think so, and here's why: Having run campaigns on three continents and in too many states to mention, we recognize how very different each unique set of circumstances is. So we've tried to focus these rules on the eternal verities, on the stuff that works anywhere.

And that itself is a lesson: Focus on the big picture. When James went to Israel to help get Ehud Barak elected prime minister, he joked that after months of research he'd concluded that the election was going to be decided by one factor: the all-important Jewish vote. But behind that joke was a larger truth: It really didn't matter so much whether the Sabbath was on a Saturday or a Sunday; the same principles apply. Speed, a culture of aggressive action, openness, empowering people, rapid response—all work across all borders.

And if the audience you're trying to reach is smaller than the one hundred million voters we spend our time trying to reach, we believe these lessons are even more important because your target audience is even more sophisticated, even more interested, even more up-to-the-minute. You should take note of the differences between our world and yours, but do not become enmeshed in them. The principles apply. The precise method of how you apply them is just one more test of your talent and creativity and flexibility.

The bottom line is that if you're faster, smarter and more aggressive than the other guy (or gal), you're going to win more often than not. The purpose of this book is to make you faster, smarter and more aggressive.

We aren't attempting to rewrite Machiavelli or Sun-tzu; no one will be studying this book five hundred years from now. But we do hope that we can give you practical, applicable strategies that will help you close a deal, land an account, get a raise, earn a promotion, win an election. And, most of all, beat your competition.

Don't Quit.
Don't Ever Quit.

THE successful politicians we've worked for and the successful leaders we've studied are a varied lot. They include the smart and . . . well . . . the not-so-smart, world-class charmers and world-class jerks, the lucky and the star-crossed. So we don't believe that brains or personality or good fortune are the most important attributes in a winner.

> Perseverance.
> Toughness.
> Tenacity.

Those are the qualities that make the difference. Real winners know they've got to lose a lot. Look at the 1998 Yankees. The year they ran up the best record in the history of baseball, they still walked off the field as losers—fifty times.[1]

You're Not as Big a Loser as Lincoln Was

Everybody fails. Everybody. Every schoolchild has heard the story of Abraham Lincoln's great accomplishments. How he saved the Union and emancipated the slaves. But you can learn more from Lincoln's failures; he certainly did. And they were far more numerous than his successes.

He failed in business (as a shopkeeper). He failed as a farmer. He ran for the state legislature—and lost. His sweetheart died. He had a nervous breakdown. When he finally got to the state legislature, he ran for Speaker—and lost. He ran for Congress—and lost. He was rejected for a job as a land officer. He ran for the United States Senate—and lost. He ran for vice president—and lost. He ran for the Senate again. Lost again. And when he was finally elected president, the nation he was elected to lead broke apart.[2]

As commander in chief Lincoln was derided as inexperienced and inept. He lost the First Battle of Manassas. He lost the Battle of Big Bethel. He lost the Battle of Kessler's Cross Lanes. And he lost at Blackburn's Ford and he lost at Ball's Bluff and he lost at McDowell and he lost at Front Royal. He lost the First Battle of Winchester and he lost at Cross Keys and he lost at Port Republic. He lost at Drewry's Bluff and he lost at Gaine's Mill and he lost at Cedar Mountain. He went on to lose at Bristoe Station and to lose at Thoroughfare Gap and to lose at the Second Battle of Manassas.

Unfazed, Lincoln pressed on. He lost at Harper's Ferry and he lost at Shepardstown (after which he fired his general). Then with a new general in charge, Lincoln proceeded to lose the First Battle of Fredericksburg.[3]

And that partial list of failures was all just in the first two years of the war. Lincoln was prone to depression. During the war his son Willie died and his wife was the subject of bitter political attacks for her allegedly spendthrift ways (including buying the famous bed that today is in the Lincoln Bedroom of the White House).

But despite all that failure Lincoln triumphed in the end.

The great Texas songwriter Kinky Friedman once warbled, "They ain't makin' Jews like Jesus anymore." And they ain't makin' politicians like Lincoln anymore either. But his lessons of toughness and tenacity are just as relevant today.

We guarantee this: If you show us a successful person, we'll show you someone who's failed. Your humble authors were abject failures at political consulting for years. James began his career as a political consultant in Louisiana after concluding he was such a poor lawyer that if he had to hire an attorney, he wouldn't hire himself.

So he went into the political-consulting business. And lost a lot. After being 0-for-life in Louisiana, James signed on to the Dick Davis for Senate campaign in Virginia.

And lost.

Then in 1984 James hooked up with the Lloyd Doggett for Senate campaign in Texas. That's where he and Paul first teamed up. And where they first lost. Big time. They suffered what up to that time was the worst defeat a Democrat had received in Texas history.

The Three-Time Loss from Holy Cross Runs a Fourth Time

Undaunted, the Carville and Begala team went on. And our careers were resurrected by a man who was then known as one of the greatest failures in his state's political history.

Bob Casey had run for governor of Pennsylvania three times—and lost three times. A devout Catholic educated by the Jesuits at Holy Cross, Casey was dismissed by the smart guys in Pennsylvania politics when he decided to try a third run for governor in 1986. He had a hard time finding a campaign manager. And as a political-consulting team that had never won a race in our career, we had a hard time finding a candidate. We were like the last two kids at a homecoming dance, homely and awkward. All the good-looking, popular, cool kids had already paired off, leaving us losers behind.

But as Casey used to say, "The view from the canvas can be highly educational." He said he didn't mind being called "the three-time loss from Holy Cross" because the name "captures something about my life and my whole idea of America itself."[4]

Casey used his previous failures, which had come at the hands of a political establishment that didn't want his independent, activist brand of government, to connect with the tough-as-nails people of his Rust Belt state. In 1986 he ran for governor a fourth time in the Democratic primary against Ed Rendell, the slick and savvy Philadelphia D.A.— and surprised the doubters by beating Rendell handily.

But in the general election Casey, who was from Scranton, was running against a Scranton. William W. Scranton III, to be exact. The movie-star-handsome scion of the legendary Pennsylvania political family and two-term lieutenant governor under the popular Republican governor Dick Thornburgh. It was, *Time* magazine wrote, like a John O'Hara story.

Casey's father, Alphonsus, had worked in the anthracite coal mines of northeastern Pennsylvania. He'd been a mule tender, a kid who led the mules hauling loads of coal out of the mines. His hands were gnarled from being run over by the heavy coal cars, but his spirit was fierce. Alphonsus

Casey had lifted himself out of those mines, gotten an education and become a lawyer. He died in his forties, leaving his son a legacy of bullheaded determination.

Young Bill Scranton's background couldn't have been more different. His father had been governor and a leader of the moderate wing of the GOP. He'd been talked about for the presidency, before the party moved to the Goldwater right. It was a classic matchup: The Scranton family had owned coal mines. The Casey family had worked in them.

After a nip-and-tuck campaign, Scranton opened up a lead in the final days by promising to stop all negative campaigning. The move was effective. The campaign had been rough, and Scranton wisely capitalized on the growing revulsion among voters. We were slow to pick up on it—in part because we were such junkyard dogs that we were having a ball in the brawl. Besides, we knew that our attacks were more powerful than our positive message.

What do you do when your most effective weapon is neutralized? If you're Bob Casey what you don't do is give up. What you don't do is give in. In this case we tried to lift the campaign out of the mud by announcing that Casey had forbidden us from making an issue out of the alleged drug use in young Scranton's past. (Of course, that little announcement *made* it an issue, but folks didn't think it counted as negative campaigning.)

Then we did the cruelest thing you can do to a politician: We held young Bill Scranton to his word. We searched every corner of the Keystone State for any sign that Scranton was secretly trashing Casey. Nothing. The election was on November 4, and on October 25, James's forty-second birthday, we went to an afternoon movie to take our minds off our misery. The movie was *Peggy Sue Got Married,* and the only thing either of us remembers about it is that James periodically burst into tears in the dark, crying, "We're gonna lose! We're gonna lose!"

With that out of our system, we returned to campaign headquarters. There, by some miracle, we heard from a supporter who'd received a piece of attack mail from the Scranton campaign that accused Casey of being part of a corrupt era of politics that had brought Pennsylvania to its knees.

The supporter was upset. We couldn't have been happier. For one thing, Casey had been the reformer who'd fought his own party's corruption for years, so we knew there'd be a backlash. But, more important, we'd caught Scranton attacking, breaking his word, acting like a hypocrite. Gleefully we counterattacked, screaming at reporters with an indignation we hoped hid our glee. We accused Scranton of pontificating on TV, while his hate message "slipped silently through the mail." (As if something ever traveled noisily through the mail.)

Scranton said he hadn't known about the mailing. Big mistake. When you're running for governor, you know or you ought to know everything your campaign is doing. And even if you don't know, you don't pass the buck. People can forgive a mistake, but they hate a weasel who tries to shift blame. Besides, this was a 600,000-piece mailing, hardly the kind of thing that falls through the cracks of a campaign.

To drive our point home, we called Billy McGrath, Casey's son-in-law who worked for a big printing house, and asked him if he could get us 600,000 envelopes and deliver them to our campaign headquarters. To this day Billy's response is the stuff of Pennsylvania political legend. He didn't ask why. He didn't ask if we were crazy. He only asked, "What color?"

Casey went on to win that race and on inauguration day we gave him a small sculpture, carved out of the same anthracite coal his father had helped to mine. It was an image of a load of coal being dragged out of a mine by a mule tender and a team of mules. At the base we'd had engraved: "To Bob Casey, the son of a mule tender who is governor today because he never gave up and never gave in."

Casey would go on to be reelected by one of the greatest landslides in Pennsylvania history—carrying sixty of the state's sixty-seven counties and defeating his Republican opponent by more than a million votes.

In any other political story that would be the happy ending. Casey's toughness and tenacity led to triumph. But his twenty-year odyssey to become governor was just a tune-up for the challenges to come. During Casey's tenure as governor he had heart bypass surgery, then he was diagnosed with a rare blood disorder that was slowly causing his heart muscle to thicken into a solid mass.

Giving up and dying quietly was not an option for Bob Casey. He found the smartest, most aggressive doctor he could, Dr. Thomas Starzl. Starzl was a pioneer in organ transplantation, and he gave Bob Casey a new heart and a new liver. Casey served his full term and is widely regarded as one of the best governors in Pennsylvania history.

Conservatives rightly remember him for his staunch commitment to his pro-life views. But they conveniently ignore Casey's lionhearted liberalism—the fact that he'd been endorsed for governor by the *Philadelphia Gay News,* that he'd pushed for strong environmental regulations, strong unions and a strong government. He created a children's health-care program that became the model for the nation, passed tough environmental laws and reformed public education.

Outside the Governor's Mansion Casey built a statue of a heroic, muscular workingman, in the style popular during the New Deal. Casey worked hard to raise the money to build it. "Because," he once told us, "I want every son of a bitch who ever lives in that house to walk out that door every morning and be reminded he works for the working people of Pennsylvania."

Even more than his political accomplishments or his public-policy contributions, Bob Casey's lasting lesson is the raw power of sheer determination. You won't believe how far you can go if you simply refuse to quit.

Where the Comeback Kid Got His Resilience

Of course, even his most ardent detractors have to admit that Bill Clinton is the king of the comeback. There are a thousand reasons why attacks that would have killed anyone else barely fazed Clinton. But if you want just one, and you want to get touchy-feely about it, you should have known his mother.

Virginia Kelly was a piece of work. Flamboyant, full of life, wide open to whatever came her way. You would never have known by talking to this Hot Springs Auntie Mame that she had been widowed before her first son was born. That her second husband had been an abusive alcoholic who once shot at her with a gun. Or that her third husband had gone to prison, then died of cancer. Or that her beloved son Roger had had a terrible bout with drug addiction, which had landed him in prison as a result of a sting operation approved by her older son. Nor would you have guessed that, during her eldest son's first term in the White House, she was dying of breast cancer and she knew it.

"The most important thing," she said to Paul toward the end, "is to never, ever become bitter. I know some people get shot up in wars and some people die. Everyone has their share of heartache. But you must never become bitter. Never, ever give in to bitterness. Because becoming bitter is giving up."

Ms. Virginia Kelly, God rest her soul, was never bitter. She was no quitter. And neither was her firstborn son. He never said it out loud—at least not to us—but we always suspected that in the darkest hours, when everyone was wondering how he could keep on going, he heard his mother telling him, "Bill, you just keep putting one foot in front of the other. The presidency is easy; life is hard." Maybe that's why Clinton always seemed so wonderfully (or, to his adversaries, maddeningly) unaffected by his tribulations. Through his mother he'd seen real pain. Impeachment is a walk in the park compared with burying three husbands and facing terminal cancer with a smile.

Put Yourself in the Position to Win

One of the reasons that people who persevere often succeed in the end is that they put themselves in a position to win. The great Mississippi singer-songwriter Steve Forbert has a song titled "You Cannot Win If You Do Not Play," and like most powerful truths, this one is simple.

The easiest way to be undefeated is to never compete. But folks who don't try, who don't fight, who don't compete are losers already.

If you're one of the people Teddy Roosevelt called "those cold and timid souls who know neither victory nor defeat,"[5] who sit on the sidelines bitching, do us a favor: Don't buy this book. If you've already bought it, thanks,

JAMES CARVILLE & PAUL BEGALA

but give it to someone who wants to get into the arena and fight.

Michael Jordan was able to hit the winning shot at the buzzer in part because he wanted the ball when the game was on the line. The other nine players on the court were skilled professionals, but none of them had the *cojones* to grab the ball, take the risk and accept the consequences. They might have missed. Hell, Jordan might have missed, too. But you miss 100 percent of the shots you don't take.

Different people have different comfort levels with risk. That's okay. We're not trying to make you into something you're not, and we're not trying to sit in judgment of people who are not as comfortable putting themselves on the line. And there's an important place in the world for people who are risk-averse. We certainly hope the doctors and nurses who have our lives in their hands are risk-averse. But then again they're taking risks with other people's lives. We're talking about taking risks not with your life—and certainly not with anyone else's life—just with your career.

Because while we know and love people with a low tolerance for risk, the stark reality is that they are people who have a low propensity for success. Again, this is not a moral judgment. James's daddy was the most risk-averse person you ever saw. He was perfectly content to spend his life as a rural postmaster. For the life of him he could not understand why James, when he was young and single, would want to drive all the way to New Orleans to drink beer and chase women with his buddies. "We've got women here in Carville," he'd say. "And we've got plenty of beer. Besides, you can't park in the French Quarter and God only knows what might happen to you."

He was so risk-averse he didn't even much like it when

28

the country would come out to fix a pothole. "They're just going to mess around and make it worse," he'd grumble.

To be fair (and accurate), Chester Carville was a success in the most important things in life: a devoted husband of thirty-five years, the father of eight children, he served as an army major in World War II and both practiced and preached racial tolerance at a time and in a place where racism was as thick as the humidity.

But this book is about politics and strategy and business and success. They are not the most important things in life. But as we said in the introduction, this ain't the Bible.

Chances are, if you bought this book, you've probably got a higher tolerance for risk than Mr. Carville did. Our hope is that we can ease that tolerance level up another notch or two. Because the odds are easy to figure: If you take more chances, you've got more chances to win. And the converse is also true: If you have a low tolerance for risk, you've got a lower probability of success.

You've probably seen this phenomenon at work in your personal life. How many times have you said "I'm not going to call that girl (or guy). Probably wouldn't go out with me anyway." Well, she (or he) is damn sure not going to go out with you if you don't ask. Back when James was a student at LSU he was smitten with a pretty young girl. She was everything he wasn't: attractive, popular, cool. James had a few classes with her, knew her casually, and she was always nice to him. More times than he can count he picked up the phone and started to call her. And more times than he can count he slammed the phone down in a panic before he dialed the last number.

Fast-forward from that campus crush of 1963 to the lecture circuit of 1997. Thirty-four years later James was giving a speech when a young woman approached him. She was attractive and cool—and strangely familiar. She said, "Mr. Carville, I don't know if you'd remember her, but my mother went to LSU with you. She said she always had a crush on you, but you never asked her out."

Jesus wept.

James, on the other hand, was reminded once more about how foolish it is to be timid. What was she going to do, that pretty and popular girl, laugh at him? Of course not. She was far too sweet and well bred to do that. But because he was terrified of rejection, James never took the risk. The fewer stories like this you have when you lay your head down at the end of your life, the happier you're going to be.

The Point

The point here is very simple. Don't quit.

It's the ultimate easier-said-than-done lesson. Nobody thinks of himself or herself as a quitter. And yet most people who fail do so because they simply give in. They get tired, or they're worn down, or they lose whatever zeal got them motivated in the first place. There's a reason pit bulls are the best fighting dogs. They're not the biggest or the strongest or the scariest. They're the most tenacious. Once they commit to taking a piece out of your leg, there's precious little on heaven or earth that can get them off you. So be a pit bull, not a Chihuahua.

You can throw the rest of this book away—and have a damn good shot at being successful in life—if you swear, right here and right now, that you'll never, ever quit. (But that would be sort of like quitting on the book, though, wouldn't it? Hmmmm. You had no idea we were capable of such existential thought, did you? It's probably best to read on, just so we won't call you a quitter.)

The Legend
of Jack LaPellerie

Of all the many legends of James's hometown of Carville, Louisiana, perhaps none has endured longer than that of Jack LaPellerie. Jack was a boilerman on the navy ship that carried President Woodrow Wilson to the signing of the Treaty of Versailles, which ended World War I.

Like virtually all of the white folks in Carville, Jack's people came from France—with a stopover in Canada. Then these Acadians made their way to Louisiana, where they're known as Cajuns. But Francophiles' love for the motherland endures, and when it was learned that Jack was actually going to France, the local French teacher and lover of all things French, Miss Mamie Grevenberg, was beside herself.

During the entire time Jack was gone, Miss Mamie breathlessly lectured anyone who would listen about the thrilling sights Jack was beholding—sights no one in that poor little burg had actually seen. So you can imagine the celebration when Jack returned from his heroic voyage. Miss Mamie rushed up to him and in her thick Cajun-French accent asked, "Jacques, tell me everything. Was the food heavenly? Is the Eiffel Tower really as high as the clouds? Is the City of Light as romantic and magical as a Victor Hugo novel?"

And Jack LaPellerie said, "Hell. I never left the boat. You don't know what could happen in a foreign country like that. Food could be spoiled or the water could make you sick. Nosirree, I stayed safe and sound on that boat."

James's grandmother loved to tell him that story with her own punch line: "And don't you ever forget, son, that ninety percent of the people around here thought Jack was right."

Rule 2

Kiss Ass

We knew this one would get your attention.

Early in his career William Faulkner had a secure job at a local post office in Mississippi. He resigned abruptly despite having no other employment prospects. When he reflected later on why he'd made such a rash move, he said, "I refused to be at the beck and call of every son of a bitch who could afford a two-cent stamp."

Guess what? You ain't Faulkner.

You're at the beck and call of every supervisor, every customer and every subordinate in your company. You're at the beck and call of every in-law, neighbor, pastor and friend. Deal with it.

The simple truth is, you never stand so tall as when you stoop to kiss an ass.

This rule is one you won't find in any of those namby-pamby, touchy-feely self-help books, but it's likely to do you more good than any of the rest of them.

What do we mean by kissing ass? That you should go through life as a shameless brownnoser, a pathetic sycophant? No. No one gets to the top strictly by sucking up. And if done clumsily, ass-kissing is a sure path to failure. Mere flattery, reflexive, obsequious praise, humiliating groveling—these are tactics for losers. What we're talking about is as different from that as Isaac Stern on a Stradavarius is from the banjo boy in *Deliverance*.

Ass-kissing is both an art and a science. No one gets to the top without learning how to deal with people you can't stand. And usually the best way to deal with them is to pretend you *can* stand them. With all due respect, we think our background in politics has given us a Ph.D. in ass-kissing. After all, politicians are at the beck and call not only of every son of a bitch who can afford a two-cent stamp, but every son of a bitch who can't afford one but has a voter registration card.

From time to time we'd get candidates—invariably first-time candidates—who'd tell us, "I don't suffer fools gladly." We'd tell them, "We do, or we wouldn't be here." Because anyone who says "I don't suffer fools gladly" is a fool himself or herself. Gladly or not, the rest of us are suffering him or her. You, dear reader, will suffer fools . . . and gladly. Because fools are all around you. Your boss, for example. Or your employees.

How 'bout your neighbor? When he asks you if he can stop by to show you the snapshots from his vacation trip to New Brunswick, New Jersey, do you say, "Hell, no, you moron. Leave me alone"? Not if you want someone to pick up your mail and feed your dog while you're on vacation, you don't.

Most of the politicians we've worked for resisted this lesson more than any of the others. And for good reason. Most were proud, intelligent, successful people—millionaire businessmen or popular senators or powerful governors or even the president of the United States. But they all had to kiss some ass to get where they wanted to go.

If it makes it easier for you, don't think of it as ass-kissing. Think of it as charm. Anytime someone says to you, "That guy sure was charming," what he's really saying is "That guy kissed my ass. I liked it. Therefore I like him."

Kiss Ass with Your Ears

The first rule of ass-kissing . . . err . . . charm is: Be a good listener. This is harder than it sounds. If you're successful, ambitious, driven, intelligent—and if you bought this book chances are you're all of those things (see: ass-kissing works!)—it's probably difficult to listen to someone else. When we say listen, we don't mean reload or catch your breath or plan your next bons mots. We don't mean feigning interest while you're actually thinking about that scene from *Basic Instinct.*

Really listen. Engage your partner nonverbally, visually and intellectually. When you listen that intently, it's difficult not to come away with a pretty good appreciation for what the other person is saying. That in itself is a subtle form of sucking up. And then, even if you disagree, chances are you'll do so in a way that shows respect for the other person's opinion.

If we had a nickel for every person who came away from meeting Bill Clinton saying, "He made me feel like the only person in the world at that moment," well, we wouldn't need the money from this book. We'd keep our secrets to success a secret as we sat on the beach in Rio. One of the great keys to Clinton's magnetic effect on people is his ability to listen. It's not a parlor trick for him, either. He really does listen. He's one of those rare people who is both hyperintelligent and always eager to learn new things. And as Mama always said, the Good Lord gave you two ears and only one mouth for a reason: You learn twice as much when you listen than when you talk.

Reciprocity Rules

The second rule of ass-kissing is that you reap what you sow. Reciprocity is a basic human emotion.

Try this experiment. Go to the person in the office next to yours and tell him or her that some third party thinks highly of him or her. "You know, Debbie, Ralph in accounting told me he thinks you're one of the brightest stars in this division." Watch Debbie's reaction. Does she say "Ralph is an idiot"? No. She says "I always thought Ralph was a good guy."

Reciprocity. We return what we receive. That's why successful politicians and other leaders have learned to send out positive messages. It starts a virtuous cycle and greases the skids for the inevitable tough times.

Turning Fools into Tools

The third rule of ass-kissing is that you should appreciate the transformative powers of the right kind of sucking up. Jesus said the poor will always be with us. But he could have said the same thing about fools. They're always going to be with us—and their identity is entirely in the eye of the beholder. Think about it. As you're reading this, certain people come to mind. They're the fools, and you're the gifted one. But believe us, someone else is reading this and thinking about you.

(If this was a partisan book, we would say that no Bush

voters can ever again say they don't suffer fools gladly, since they helped put one in the White House. But this is not a partisan book, so we wouldn't dream of taking such a potshot.)

If your only way to handle people you think are fools is by belittling them, you're going to be awfully lonely. It's easy to berate someone. But it takes an enormous amount of creativity, energy and leadership to bring someone along with you who perhaps doesn't get it at first. And if you're really good, maybe one day that fool will get it. He will begin to understand what you're trying to do, and since you've involved him in the process, he's bought in to the objective, the strategy and the tactic. Voilà, he's not a fool anymore. He may not be a genius, but he's not the dead-weight he would have been if you hadn't suffered him gladly—and transformed him out of his foolhardiness.

If you think your organization is too autocratic for this kind of sucking up, you're wrong. James tried this theory on the toughest cookies in the world, the United States Marine Corps—and it worked. In a speech at the Marine War College he spelled out why even officers in the Corps have to suffer fools gladly. After his lecture more than one battle-hardened Marine officer told him he was right. There is simply no way to get by in this world without dealing with fools.

Those Marines understood that making a decision is the easy part. Making it stick is hard. Putting a decision into effect across a company or a campaign or any other culture takes more than one person. Anyone can pull a lever. But to make something happen, that lever has to be attached to ropes and pulleys and winches and cranes and all manner of machinery.

Inanimate objects don't have the capacity to resist or re-sent, to ignore or undermine. But people do. So a good leader "buys folks into the process." She buys their support with a currency more valuable than dollars and cents: time and attention. She includes them in the process, making them feel valued and valuable. All of that is just a fancy way of saying that a good leader knows the strategic use of ass-kissing.

Motivate, Don't Dictate

It may be too early in this book to tell you this, but what the hell. You've already paid for it; you may as well get the truth up front. The truth is, we're not political geniuses. There are no political geniuses—or at least there are damn few of them. Okay, once in a generation a Roosevelt or a Kennedy or a Clinton comes along (you Republicans can also claim your own Roosevelt, and Reagan, if you like). But the painful truth is, we are no better than at least one hundred other professional political strategists in the business today.

So why do we get fat book contracts, lucrative lecture deals and endless hours on television? Luck? Yes. But also because of this: What separates the handful of top political strategists from all the rest is the same thing that separates the top business executives from all the rest. And it ain't brains, and it ain't luck, and it damn sure ain't looks. It's the ability to get people to execute the strategy we come up with.

Knowing what to do is not that hard. What separates the successful from the mediocre is the ability to get other people to do what you need them to do. And if you think you can get people—especially intelligent, talented, creative people—to do what you want simply through threats and intimidation, you're wrong. Try that and you'll be about as successful as you'd be shoveling steam.

The idea that you can just tell people "Go do *X*," and they just do it is a myth. They may do it. But they'll probably do it in a half-assed way or do it without enthusiasm— or they might leave you and do it for someone who treats them better.

You have to sell your own people on what you're doing before you can sell anyone else. The most important people with whom we communicated in the 1992 Clinton presidential campaign were not the contributors, not the media, or even the one hundred million Americans who were going to vote. It was the fifty people on our staff who were responsible for getting our message out to the one hundred million people who were going to be voting.

If you're the parent of a small child, you can get away with saying "Because I'm the parent and I say so" for a while. But if you treat your people like they're small children, they'll leave you—just like your children will when they are old enough to think for themselves. The difference is that the purpose of parenting is to prepare those young'uns to leave. But the purpose of leadership is to get adults—smart, competent adults—to stay with you and to follow you. You've got to create a culture, a philosophy that makes people feel as if they're part of something important—and that they themselves are important.

We used to do crazy things to motivate people during our campaigns. The first campaign we did together was for Lloyd Doggett for U.S. Senate. It was 1984 in Texas. Ronald Reagan would have beaten Jesus Christ in Texas in 1984, and Phil Gramm was Ronald Reagan's favorite Texan. We had fought hard and cleverly for the Democratic nomination, and we intended to fight to the death for the victory, but with each passing day it appeared that the Reagan landslide over Mondale was going to produce a bit of a Gramm tsunami over Doggett.

James was the campaign manager and he faced the difficult task of motivating a staff that was bright enough to read the writing on the wall. One Friday evening, when things were going particularly badly, James gathered the staff together, gave everyone a couple of beers and selected one of the young people—the kind of guy who might lose heart in a losing campaign—and told him he'd pay him one hundred dollars if he could crack three eggs over his head. The guy—his name was George and he had moved from North Carolina to Texas to help us out—was dubious. So he got the campaign's in-house lawyer to draft a contract that said that James Carville agreed to pay George one hundred dollars if Carville cracks three eggs on George's head. So the whole staff gathered around to witness the event.

C-r-a-c-k went the first egg. The yolk and the white streamed down George's face and the staff went wild.

C-r-a-c-k went the second egg. George couldn't contain his glee at the prospect of earning an extra hundred bucks—but really at being the center of attention.

And then . . . nothing.

"Awww, the hell with it," James said. "I don't really feel like doing three." And he walked away. Right on cue the campaign lawyer told George, "There's nothing in this contract that says he's got to give you a dime for just two eggs." So George wound up pleading for the third egg, begging James to crack another egg over his head. James demurred, handing George a beer instead and telling him to go clean himself up and request a refund from his college professors.

The staff was rolling with laughter. James had shown

them that if he could be a clown, maybe things weren't so bad after all. It did more good than a thousand screaming locker-room-style speeches; it built an esprit de corps that forged lifelong friendships. Those young people gave every ounce of their energy to a hopeless cause for the next several months.

You don't have to be that mischievous, though. On that same famous sign that said IT'S THE ECONOMY, STUPID, we also had a space for Employee of the Week. To have your name placed on that sign was worth more than all the meager pay we could offer.

And one of the best motivators we had in the War Room was the gold star. We're not making this up. Like a preschool teacher, James would stop the morning or evening War Room meeting and ostentatiously stick a gold star on the forehead of a staff member who had done a particularly outstanding job. We're not talking about three-year-olds here. We're talking about George Stephanopoulos and Gene Sperling (who went on to become President Clinton's top economic adviser); Michael Waldman (who became Clinton's chief speechwriter) and Bob Boorstin (who held top posts in the White House, the State Department and the Treasury Department), Ricki Seidman (who was a top aide in the White House and the Justice Department) and Eric Berman (who has gone on to a stellar career as a Wall Street strategist). The most brilliant people of their generation would run through walls to get a gold star with James's slobber on it stuck to their forehead.

That's not to say the staff was never criticized. Standards were uncompromising, and those who failed to live up to them were told so in no uncertain terms. Many's the bright young Ivy Leaguer who had to endure a tirade that began like this: "How much did your parents waste on sending

you to Harvard, kid? They oughta sue 'em for malpractice."
Even the most dedicated ass-kisser has to know when it's
time to become an ass-kicker (wait till Rule Three).

The Imus Touch

Perhaps no one we know has better perfected the strategic
balance between kissing ass and kicking ass than Don
Imus. The legendary radio host is a study in contradictions:
a vegetarian who owns a cattle ranch, a misanthrope who
spends his time and money helping children who have cancer, an outsider who is the toast of the Washington punditocracy. Listen to *Imus in the Morning* for any length of time
and you get a sense of the man's mastery.

Take Imus's relationship to Bill Clinton, for example.
Imus regularly abused Clinton in the 1992 primaries. He
called him Butterbutt, Bubba and worse. Then one day,
prodded in part by Joe Lieberman and Bill Bradley (and,
yes, we admit, your authors are big Imus fans and told Clinton so), Clinton called in to the program. Imus seemed a little sheepish about some of the name-calling he'd engaged
in until Clinton zinged him with this: "I don't mind. Bubba's
just southern for mensch."

Instantly, Clinton was an I-fave. They've had their ups
and downs since then, but Imus's combination of abuse
and flattery was nothing short of masterful—and Clinton's
comeback wasn't too bad, either.

By the 2000 election, Imus was a major force in the
media. Named one of the twenty-five Most Influential People in America by *Time* magazine in 1997, Imus engaged in
a strange courtship of Al Gore. For months—even years—
Imus savaged Gore, calling him (among other things) "the
single most evil person on the face of the planet." Perhaps

tiring of the abuse, or perhaps in the hopes of turning Imus the way Clinton had, Gore consented to an interview. Within moments of announcing he'd landed Gore, Imus was referring to him as "my man, Al." This despite the fact that he'd already endorsed Imus regulars Bill Bradley and John McCain for president.

In the interview with Gore, Imus hit the veep right between the eyes with tough questions like why Gore had taken tobacco money even after his sister had died of cancer. But he also covered a wide variety of policy issues. And he got Gore to relax enough to show his rarely seen but very sharp sense of humor.

After he finished the Imus interview, Gore told Paul that "that was the most substantive interview I've had so far in this campaign." Apparently it helps if behind the staged abuse and the mock sucking up you know what the hell you're doing. And Don Imus certainly does. (How's *that* for practicing what we preach?)

The Point

We know they *say* no one likes a brownnoser. But have you ever had someone tell you, "I don't like Sylvia. She's always kissing my ass"? No. People gripe about ass-kissers because *their* ass is not getting kissed. So pucker up. Be strategic about it. Don't be a drooling, fawning fool. But if what it takes to keep a subordinate on the team, or keep the boss in the program, is a little extra time and attention when you'd really rather be telling him or her how much smarter you are, start smooching. The ass you save may be your own.

The Ass-Kissers' Hall of Fame

Here are a couple of examples of politicians who smooched to conquer.

- **John Fitzgerald Kennedy:** Although he won the Pulitzer Prize for *Profiles in Courage,* our war hero president was not above puckering up when it served his interests. He was deeply suspicious of Lyndon Johnson, and his brother Robert plainly hated LBJ. But with the election in doubt, he asked the Texan to join the ticket. Kennedy knew he couldn't have both his pride and the presidency. History shows that he made the right choice.

  Later, when his dream of putting a man on the moon was in jeopardy, Kennedy agreed to locate mission control not in his native Massachusetts but rather in Houston. Why? Because Houston congressman Albert Thomas controlled the committee that controlled the funding. One of humanity's greatest achievements was made possible only because the most powerful man on the face of the earth was willing to kiss the ass of a congressman you've never heard of.

- **Ronald Wilson Reagan:** Perhaps the smoothest brownnoser we ever had in the White House, Reagan could charm and manipulate on a world-class level. He fawned over British prime minister Margaret Thatcher with a seductive skill that must have made her husband, Dennis, a tad nervous. While Reagan's secretary of state, Alexander Haig, was trying to mediate in the Falklands War (which was fought between two American allies, Argentina and

Great Britain, over a group of islands three hundred miles off the Argentine coast in the South Atlantic), Reagan shut down Haig's evenhanded diplomacy and sided with Britain, imposing sanctions against Argentina despite Argentina's support of American anticommunist activity in Latin America.

Thatcher won the war and forevermore served as an intellectual supporter and international cheerleader for Reagan, which she remains to this day. A short-term suck-up has paid dividends for decades.[1]

The Ass-Kissers' Hall of Shame

Of course, there are counterexamples as well; times when oafish, Eddie Haskell–like politicians have hurt themselves and their cause by kissing ass in a way that was obvious and weak. But there is one ass-kisser in a class by himself.

- **Neville Chamberlain:** His very name conjures up an image of weakness, and for good reason. It's all well and good to kiss ass to a congressman or an ally, a boss or a customer, but it's going a little far when you suck up to the most evil man in history, Adolf Hitler. The Conservative British prime minister thought Hitler was someone he could "appease." So after Hitler had re-armed the Rhineland, in violation of the Treaty of Versailles (the treaty that ended World War I), and after he had "annexed" Austria (also in violation of the Treaty of Versailles), Chamberlain cut a deal with Hitler: the infamous Munich Accord of September 1938. In it Chamberlain agreed to allow Hitler to take over a large chunk of Czechoslovakia, known as the Sudetenland, despite the rather strenuous objections of the Czechs.[2]

  After kowtowing to Hitler, Chamberlain declared, "A British Prime Minister has returned from Germany bringing peace with honour. I believe it is peace for our time. . . . Go home and get a nice quiet sleep."[3]

  Hitler, of course, did not go home and get a nice quiet sleep. He invaded the rest of Czechoslovakia, then

Poland, Denmark and Norway. Then he invaded France, Belgium, Luxembourg and the Netherlands. At that point Chamberlain resigned and Winston Churchill took over. But not before Chamberlain's appeasement had helped plunge the world into its bloodiest war.

Rule 3

Kick Ass

An All-or-Nothing Game

Now that we've sold you on the virtues of coopting people, we don't want you to think that sucking up is the only way to win. In fact, it's just one of several tactical weapons you can deploy.

There are times when a foe is implacable and the choice is mutually exclusive: *A and not B.* An election is a perfect example. You can legally buy a can of Pepsi and a can of Coke at the same time. But you can't vote for Bush and Gore for president on the same day; it's impossible—unless, of course, you live in Florida. But even there your vote will probably go to Buchanan anyway.

Voting is a mutually exclusive choice. That's why politics is so often negative; it's an all-or-nothing game. Believe us, if you could only buy one brand of soft drink—and you were stuck with your choice for four years—the cola wars would make political combat look like a Girl Scout jamboree.

Coke's ad would say:

Pepsi. The Choice of a New Generation . . . of Cancer-Infested Rats. That's right. In a scientific study, rats that drank Pepsi became riddled with cancer—pretty much immediately. Coke, on the other hand, did not cause cancer in rats. So the choice is yours: Drink Coke and live—or drink Pepsi and die a slow, painful death.

And Pepsi would counter:

Ever see those hopeless souls shuffling behind shopping carts, mumbling to themselves? Unwashed, unloved—very uncool. You probably thought it was drugs or alcohol or mental illness, right? Think again. It was Coca-Cola. Turns out Coke makes you break out in ugly zits. It also makes you fat. And smelly. Pretty soon no one wants to be around you. And forget about getting laid. So you wind up shooting smack in an alley with a guy named Pony Boy. Pepsi, on the other hand, is the official soft drink of Britney Spears. Your choice, America: smelly, crazy crackheads who never get laid—or Britney Spears.

A campaign—or any other ongoing, dynamic enterprise—is like riding a bike: the more forward momentum you have, the harder it is to knock you over. But if you're just barely moving, or trying to stand still, even the slightest push will make you tumble.

Sound obvious? That's because it is. And yet it's astonishing how many people ignore the obvious. There's a saying in Spanish that gets it right: *La libertad no es tad. Es toca.* Liberty is not given. It's taken. And so are most of the important things in life.

Be aggressive. In politics that translates into one word: attack.

We love negative campaigning. Not what President Clinton memorably dubbed "the politics of personal destruction," but hard-hitting, above-the-belt, smash-mouth attacks. Voters love it, too—the louder the better. And although some of the blowhards in the media decry it, they're the same people who put sex scandals on page one.

The nature of the press is one reason we believe in aggressive politics. Roger Ailes, the political mastermind who helped give us Nixon, Reagan and Bush I (hey, we may not like his ideology, but we've gotta admire his talent) and who now heads the Fox News Network, has what he calls the "Orchestra Pit Theory of Press Coverage." If a politician called the media to announce he'd found a cure for cancer and then fell into the orchestra pit at the press conference, the headline would be POLITICIAN FALLS INTO ORCHESTRA PIT.

Why? Because, according to Ailes, the press likes to cover only four things in politics: scandals, gaffes, polls and attacks. Three of them are bad. So if you want to get in the paper, get your butt on the offensive and keep it there.

It is possible to be both hard-hitting and have a soft touch. It's not easy, but it is possible. Ronald Reagan was the master of being aggressive without being unpleasant. To this day, too many of his Republican successors are snarling pit bulls, lemon-sucking puritans or smirking plutocrats.

Being aggressive applies even more strongly when you aren't able to get in the first shot. If your opponent's initial punch is aggressive, your response had better be twice as aggressive. To quote Sean Connery's brilliant speech in *The Untouchables:* "You wanna know how to nail Capone? This is how you nail Capone: he pulls a knife, you pull a gun, he puts one of yours in the hospital, you put one of his in the morgue. *That's* how you nail Capone."

Amen, Sean.

The Counterpunch Kid

If Reagan was the master of killing with kindness, Bill Clinton was the king of the counterpunch. As every good boxer knows, a counterpunch can sometimes be more punishing than an initial blow. That's because a good counterpuncher anticipates where the attack is coming from, understands that the attack itself leaves the opponent vulnerable to counterattack, then, with a lethal combination of speed and power, exploits that temporary vulnerability to deliver a wallop. An effective counterpuncher not only scores points, he or she demoralizes the opponent by being faster, smarter and more forceful. In the ring a classic counterpunch is to answer a slow left jab with a fast, punishing overhand right. The opponent's jab will be blunted by your right arm. Meanwhile your right fist will be doing a little dance on your opponent's face.[1]

Here's how we've seen counterpunching work in politics: In the early debates of the 1992 primaries, Clinton was loath to attack Jerry Brown. He and Brown had been governors together, and Clinton respected Brown's intellect and passion. Besides, Brown's voters were crunchy-granola liberals. Clinton's targets were white moderates and African Americans. So Clinton had a no-first-strike policy. But when, in a debate in Chicago, Brown accused Hillary Clinton of profiting from state business (a scurrilous lie that Brown said he'd been fed by Ralph Nader), Clinton struck back with a vengeance.

"How dare you jump on my wife like that!" Clinton

snarled. "You're not fit to stand on the same stage with her." Brown looked like a bully; Clinton looked like a chivalrous hero who'd fight for you as hard as he did for his wife.

And from there the legend grew. The Comeback Kid counterpunched his way out of jams no one thought he could survive.

First Impressions DO Matter More

Another reason why being aggressive is so important is that, as your mama taught you, "you never get a second chance to make a first impression." The first take really counts for a lot. The first inning of a baseball game or the first quarter of a football game is often more important than anything else. Because that's when you establish yourself.

Like every red-blooded male in the South, we played football. And one of the things the coaches taught us was that on the opening kickoff you should pick someone out on the other team and hit him just as hard as you could (which for us wasn't all that hard, but we got the idea). Doing that told that kid—and his teammates—that we were aggressive. Maybe back 'em up a step or two; make 'em think twice before they messed with you.

At least in sports the rules stay the same throughout the game. So if you're down three runs in the first inning or down 7–0 in the first quarter, you can come back by playing the game. In the real world, whether it's combat, campaigning or cold calling, if you start out on the wrong foot, it takes a long time to overcome it. Your subsequent mistakes have an exponential effect—they further legitimize the first impression, they compound your problem. So every step is uphill from then on. The rules have changed for you. You're screwed.

Here's an example. What do you think of the Denver airport? Delays, malfunctions and foul-ups galore, right? Bag-eating machines. Technology run amok. Travelers stranded. That's all because it had a tough start. The truth is, after several years in operation, it has one of the best records in the country. It makes money and has by far the best on-time record of any cold-weather airport in the world. The folks who built that airport lost the initial battle for public opinion. And the consequences have set them back years.

Same with the Hubble telescope. At first it didn't work—and it was the butt of more jokes than there are stars in the sky. But after some repairs it now gives NASA scientists the most breathtaking images of space ever captured. Try telling that to people who're not rocket scientists and they'll laugh at you. Why? Because it started out with a screwup. First impressions last.

One of the most famous cases of a poor introduction being fatal is Dan Quayle. He may not have been the brightest guy in the Senate when Bush senior picked him to be his running mate, but he wasn't the dumbest, either. He had as bad a debut on the national stage as you could have—and he never recovered from it. Quayle's first impression as a dim bulb created a master narrative so that his every mistake compounded his problem. And, God bless him, he made a lot of them.

Information technology has made the first take more important than ever. Because once a news story is filed, it is forevermore available through computer-assisted research devices like LexisNexis. Nowadays too many reporters are not really reporters; they're repeaters. Their editors order them to jump on a story, and the first thing they do is punch up what everyone else has written on it. This makes that first impression all the more important, because it becomes the basis, the starting point for every subsequent story.

Take Whitewater—please. *The New York Times* is the best newspaper in the world, but it blew the initial take on the Whitewater story. The *Times* was the first paper to report on Whitewater back in March of 1992. In its initial story the *Times* said that as governor, Bill Clinton had gone into business with an S&L operator (whose business the state regulated); that Clinton had put little or no money up but stood to gain greatly. A classic sweetheart deal. Trouble is, the story was wrong in nearly every particular.

Clinton was not yet the governor of Arkansas when he got into the Whitewater land deal. His business partner was not yet an S&L owner. Clinton did invest money in it— indeed, he lost money in the venture—and he stood to gain no more than his investment entitled him to gain.

Whoops.

Try putting *that* toothpaste back in the tube. It's bad enough when *The New York Times* gets it wrong. But it's crippling when that error is compounded time after time. Every subsequent reporter, editor, commentator, pundit, analyst and opposition researcher began his or her look into Whitewater with the *Times* original—and inaccurate—story. It took six years and $50 million before the Clintons ever fully cleared their name.

George W. Bush has learned how important first impressions are. He's one of the best first dates in American politics. Take his tax cut, for example. When they released their tax cut proposal, the Bush campaign made a deal with a few favored reporters from the major media: We will leak to you the details of our tax plan, if—and only if—you will agree not to interview anyone critical of it for twenty-four hours. That "gag rule" ensured that the initial stories on the

Bush tax plan had headlines like this one, from the astonishingly gullible *Washington Post:*

BUSH TO OFFER $483 BILLION TAX CUT PLAN
WORKING POOR, MIDDLE CLASS WOULD GET MUCH RELIEF

Here's the lead of that *Post* puff piece:

December 1, 1999—Texas Governor George W. Bush will propose a $483 billion tax cut plan today that would focus its deepest reductions on the working poor and middle class and become the centerpiece of the Republican frontrunner's economic plan.

The Bushies couldn't have gotten a better story if they'd written it themselves—because they basically did. Never mind that the true size of the tax cut was $1.6 trillion over ten years—Bush aides knew that would sound too large, so they gave the *Post* a phony five-year cost number, even though tax cuts have always been calculated over a ten-year period.

But the thing that pleased Team Bush the most was how the *Post* swallowed their line about their tax plan being for the working poor and the middle class. That crock of sheep dip was provably false—if the *Post* had done the slightest bit of homework or called a single expert in tax policy who was not on Bush's payroll. But the *Post* had made a deal with the devil. It had promised not to talk to any of the Bush plan's critics, thus guaranteeing W a clean, uncritical and completely false first impression. The *Post* kept its word. It ran the Bush campaign's tax proposal as if it was on the level—and as if the *Post* was nothing more than a stenographer for the Bush spin machine.

The truth—as we all now know—is that the Bush tax cut will cost this country trillions, and nearly half of all its benefits will go to the hyperrich, the wealthiest 1 percent of all Americans. Far from targeting the underprivileged, the Bush plan gives no tax relief at all to millions and millions of Americans who work but are poor. But none of these facts made it into the initial story because of the unholy deal the *Post* and others made, so Bush got a terrific first take on his biggest issue.

We don't blame the Bush campaign for pulling this stunt. It's more audacious—and mendacious—than even the most outrageous spin doctoring we ever did in the Clinton era. But we do blame the *Post* for running as the first, and most important, take on a critical issue what can only be described as a George W. Bush press release.

The Bush team dominated that all-important first take on their tax proposal for one reason: They were aggressive. They kicked ass, made ridiculous demands and got what they wanted. They had a plan and put it into action. In a way, we admire that.

Putting the Onus on Action

With so much riding on the first take, being aggressive is key. Or, as we liked to say in campaigns, "It's hard for your opponent to say much when your fist is in his face."

The War Room was designed for action. (No, not that kind of action. Stop snickering.) In fact, before Hillary gave it its more famous name, we called it the CAT—the Clinton Action Team. We gladly deferred to Hillary's more colorful moniker, however (see the lesson on kissing ass to understand why).

In the past, campaigns were rigid hierarchies. They were

eleven-story buildings, with the grassroots folks on the bottom floor and layers and layers of intermediary authority until, finally, you got to the top, where the decisions were made. So if an idea wanted to make its way from the bottom to the top, by the time it got to the guy with the secret key to the executive washroom, there were ten floors of functionaries who saw it as their duty to kill it.

The old structure was designed not to give momentum to ideas but to give resistance to them. They used to say that Willie Mays's glove was where triples go to die. Bureaucracies are where good ideas go to die. And big campaigns, especially presidential campaigns, become big bureaucracies. Bill and Hillary Clinton were determined that that would not happen during the 1992 campaign. So they created the War Room.

The War Room philosophy was to move the onus from the originator of the idea to the resister of the idea. We'd start the day at a 7:30 A.M. meeting in which some action would be proposed. We'd say, "Absent some compelling reason not to, presented to us by 9 A.M., we're going to do X." Then everyone on the entire staff knew the top priority: action.

That's not to say that there weren't times when those ninety minutes weren't valuable. Lots of bad ideas were killed. But if an idea is good enough to withstand ninety minutes of scrutiny from some of the toughest, smartest people in the country, it was probably a pretty good idea.

Let us give you an example. In the old days people would sit around and say, "We need to bolster our image on the economy." Then one person would say, "Let's do a labor event," and the person responsible for courting small business would say, "No, that'll piss off small business. Let's do a small business event." And every idea that was generated would be subject to death by a single argument. It was like what the United Nations would be if every country got a veto. Anything Aruba wanted to do, Azerbaijan would veto; anything Canada initiated, Congo would kill.

There are petty rivalries and turf wars in every organization, but you can't let them cripple you. So we changed the structure to shift the onus. Every department within the campaign had a representative in the War Room: the research and political and press and policy and media and polling and speechwriting teams were at the heart of it, but the administrative and fundraising and legal folks were there, too.

So the 7:30 meeting would start not with some open-ended whine about how we needed more credibility on the economy but rather with a specific idea: We are going to give a speech on the economy at the Detroit Economic Club, and absent some compelling reason not to—a reason presented by 9 A.M. at the latest, so the idea couldn't die of inertia—that speech is happening.

And a compelling reason is not "It might not work." No shit, it might not work. Let's make it work. The person who said "It might not work" was then charged with *making* it work. We tried to make our folks feel like a pit crew at the Indianapolis 500. Yes, we need new tires and, yes, we need more gas. And, yes, it needs to be done flawlessly; we can't afford to blow a tire at 200 miles per hour. But most of all we've got to get our ass on the track *moving* at 200 miles per hour. So get it done, get it done right and get it done fast.

Reward Risk More Than You Punish Failure

It's one thing to preach risk taking, quite another to make it part of your culture. If you want your organization to be action-oriented, however, you've got to reward risk taking—even unsuccessful risk taking—more than you punish failure. One of the reasons bureaucrats are so risk-averse—whether they're in an HMO blindly denying needed care or at the Department of Motor Vehicles making you fill out the same form a third time—is because the nature of most bureaucracies is to punish failure more than to reward success. It's simple behavior modification. If you give a rat one pellet for performing a difficult task well, then give it two shocks for performing it poorly, chances are that the poor rat is going to sit on its ass and do nothing; the pain of two shocks outweighs the gain of one pellet.

People are just like rats. (We didn't mean it the way it came out, but you catch our drift.) One of the best things about working for Bill Clinton was that he rewarded risk taking, and he was light in punishing those who erred while taking chances.

The morning after the New Hampshire primary, Paul was on the campaign plane heading south, aggressively spinning Adam Nagourney (then of *USA Today,* now of the *New York Times*). Paul was belittling the New Hampshire victory of Paul Tsongas, trying to argue that Clinton's death-defying comeback was a bigger story. Hoping perhaps to inspire a little negative coverage on Tsongas, Paul accused the press of "puffing" Tsongas up, then predicted, "You live by the puff, you die by the puff. That son of a bitch has lived by the puff, and now . . ."[2]

Nagourney faithfully recorded Paul's comment. Word for word. And the next morning Paul was profanely attacking Tsongas in America's Family Newspaper. His colleagues on the campaign were, shall we say, vexed. Paul's profanity sidetracked the campaign for a crucial day, allowed Tsongas to adopt the pose of the wounded, aggrieved party and gave the reporters traveling with Clinton something to write about other than what we wanted them to write about.

Clinton asked Paul if he'd said it. Paul assured him that he had but had naively hoped the reporter would clean up the language. Clinton took two measures in response to the error. First he ordered Paul to send a handwritten letter of apology to Tsongas. Then, once Paul'd done that, Clinton threw his arm around him and said, "Listen, everybody makes mistakes. I don't want you to let this take you out of your game. I like that you're in there swinging for me."

Rather than being disheartened, Paul was ready to run through a wall for Clinton all over again. A more risk-averse campaign would have reassigned Paul to administrative duties or sweeping the floor in the Duluth headquarters. But such a move would have done much more harm than good. Not only would Paul have frozen his Texas ass off in Duluth, every other person in the campaign with an aggressive attitude would have been chilled into inaction. Creating a gunshy culture is not the way to win.

Winners Do. Losers Meet.

Absent a major peace negotiation, a complicated merger or a complex legal settlement, there is no reason on earth to have any meeting last more than thirty minutes. (James would say ten, but he has a chronically short attention span. Paul has been able to stretch it out to thirty, but no longer.) The integrated structure of the War Room made lengthy, multiple meetings unnecessary. We didn't have to stop everything to run it by the research folks; the research folks were represented there. Everyone was represented there.

Sir Isaac Newton figured out something profound about

human nature as well as physics when he theorized that bodies in motion tend to stay in motion and bodies at rest tend to stay at rest—unless overcome by a more powerful force. Our goal was to overcome the inertia of analysis, put bodies in motion and make it incumbent upon those who wanted to stop that motion to offer a powerful rational to do so.

Of course, it's a fine line between aggressive and offensive, between self-confident and self-destructive. But our experience is that most of us don't live on that line. Most folks live their lives very comfortably on the safe side of risk, and that's fine, so long as they don't want to win very often. But your chances—of landing that big deal, getting that big raise, earning that big promotion, winning that big account—will increase dramatically if you adopt a more aggressive posture. That way, even if you fail, you'll know you've done your damnedest.

Attack, Dammit, Attack

Once you've decided that you need to fight—that the battle is worth waging and the price of victory is worth paying—attack. Military history is replete with stories of generals who didn't want to fight. They're called *losers*.

General George B. McClellan was a master at training troops. He was known to be an able strategist. He was beloved by his men. He had only one problem: He didn't want to attack. He kept the Army of the Potomac camped on the Potomac, training, adding men, doing everything but fighting. President Abraham Lincoln visited his hesitant general, but McClellan insisted that Robert E. Lee's Army of Northern Virginia had him vastly outnumbered and that an attack would be disastrous. Finally, in exasperation, Lincoln wrote his general: "My dear McClellan: If you don't want to use the Army I should like to borrow it for a while. Yours respectfully, A. Lincoln."[3]

Contrast McClellan's pusillanimous attitude with one of the great attack-dog generals of all time: George S. Patton. As he led his Third Army toward Berlin in World War II, Patton received word from his superior, General Omar Bradley, that he was not to take the German city of Trier. Bradley reasoned that the city would take three divisions and Patton had only two, so he told Patton to hold off.

But the hard-charging Patton had already taken Trier. His reply to Bradley was classic: "Have already taken city, do you want me to give it back?"[4]

Planning is important. Strategy is vital. Thinking through the consequences of both victory and defeat is crucial. Training and preparation are essential.

But at some point you gotta pull the damn trigger. Patton knew that.

And when you do pull the trigger, you can't hesitate. As a teenager, Paul once worked with a man who'd done time in prison. His name was Joe, and Paul, being a teenager, was fascinated to learn everything about prison life (okay, not *every*thing, just the violent parts). Joe was not a violent guy. He was a skinny, bookish man who'd been sent up the river for embezzlement. But the lesson he taught Paul has stayed with him all these years: "If you ever pull a weapon on someone," he said, holding up a piece of pipe, "you'd better use it. 'Cause if you're not perfectly willing to use it—to kill the guy if you have to—I can guarantee you he's going to take it away from you and kill you without a second thought."

The Point

Fortunately, we've never had to put Joe's advice to the literal test. But once you decide to attack, you'd better go after it with all that you've got. The person who hesitates is not only lost, he or she's dead meat. You've got to be smart about it, but smart and aggressive must go hand in hand. If your intelligence crosses the line into hesitancy, you're doomed. The time for thinking, for planning, for strategizing, is before the first punch is thrown. After that, whoever is more agile, mobile and (especially) hostile is the one who's going to walk away a winner.

There's an old saying: When you come to a fence you're not sure you can climb, throw your hat over it. Once you're committed to a course of action, you have no choice but to see it through with everything you have.

So be aggressive, be aggressive, be aggressive. You'll make your share of mistakes. But you'll win more than your share of fights.

Speed Kills (Your Opponent)

Let's talk about speed.

In politics there are two kinds of campaigns: the quick and the dead. Same thing in business or pretty much any endeavor in life. One of the biggest problems smart politicians and business leaders have is that they tend to suffer from what the Reverend Jesse Jackson calls "the paralysis of analysis." They're so smart they can always see the other side; they can always analyze potential pitfalls and problems.

The process of analysis itself takes time—and that's time well spent. But when analysis leads only to the conclusion that you need further analysis, look out. You're heading into paralysis mode.

Harry Truman understood that. He once said he was looking for a one-armed adviser, because he was sick of Washington sharpies telling him, "On the other hand . . ."

And John F. Kennedy understood something even more important: that delaying a decision is itself a decision; a decision with risks as well. "There are risks and costs to a program of action," he once said, "but they are far less than the long range risks and costs of comfortable inaction."[5]

You want to be the smartest person at the big meeting? Be the first person to demand that your organization move quickly. Acknowledge the risks and costs of doing something, then outline the myriad risks and manifest costs of doing nothing. You'll find that JFK was right.

Do something . . . now. If it works, do more of it. If it doesn't work, do something else. But do something—quickly.

The ability to access and retrieve information quickly has revolutionized the campaign business as much as it has every other business. But campaigns have adapted more quickly than some, perhaps because of the all-or-nothing nature of the enterprise. News cycles are compressed. As speed and accuracy increase, so does the effectiveness of a campaign.

Putting a premium on speed forces a premium on other virtues: accuracy, agility, flexibility. We're always amazed, whether it's in a governmental bureaucracy, a campaign bureaucracy or a corporate bureaucracy, that there is actually a correlation between speed and excellence. Most folks will tell you that moving too quickly invites mistakes, and sometimes that's true. But, more often, placing a premium on speed gives a sense of urgency and importance to the task, thus reducing errors.

In contrast, an attitude of "mañana" often breeds mistakes by conveying the notion that the task isn't all that important anyway. So if you want something done right, tell your people to do it right away.

The War Room became famous for its rapid response— for good reason. Even as President George Bush I was delivering his acceptance speech to the GOP convention in Houston, the War Room staff was faxing a point-by-point rebuttal to every reporter in America. During the debates we took to issuing "prebuttals." So familiar were we with Bush's record and rhetoric that we wanted the press to have our response to his assertions before he'd even made them.

But even more than the famous rapid response, the War Room was a place that believed in rapid initiation. After all, as Patton taught, "The object of war is not to die for your country. It's to make the other poor son of a bitch die for his country."[6] The object of a campaign is not merely to answer all of the opponent's attacks. It's to make the opponent go crazy trying to answer all of your attacks.

Rule 4

Frame the Debate

MILITARY strategists know that most battles are won before the first shot is fired—by the side that determines where, when and how an engagement is fought. Nobody wanted to fight the British at sea. But the British shouldn't have fought the American colonists in the wilds and woods of the New World.

Political professionals call the act of defining the terrain of engagement "framing the debate." In 1980, when Governor Ronald Reagan of California challenged President Jimmy Carter, Reagan's attacks on Carter's foreign policy, his economic policy and his energy policy served two purposes. They put Carter on the defensive, of course, but, more important, they framed the choice the voters had to make. Just before the election, Reagan explicitly framed the choice when he memorably asked the country: "Are you better off than you were four years ago?"

Boom. There's the frame. Most big decisions can turn on a multiplicity of points. Being aggressive helps to force the decision point to the terrain most favorable to you. Carter tried to shift the decision point to nuclear war, suggesting that Reagan was a trigger-happy cowboy who'd blow up the world, but when he tried to illustrate it by quoting his young daughter, Amy, it was hardly compelling.

Think of the decision point as a one-foot-square frame and the choice itself as a wall-size mural. Your job is to place that frame on the one square foot that's most favorable to you and least favorable to your opponent. Reagan placed that frame squarely on the issue of economic well-being. Carter tried to place it on nuclear annihilation. The voters liked Reagan's frame better, and the rest is history.

We saw the same thing in the fight over impeachment. Over and over again the folks leading the anti-Clinton charge chanted, "It's not about sex." But folks knew better. The pro-impeachment forces tried hard to place the frame on allegations of perjury and the like, while Clinton defenders said that while he'd been a rotten husband he was a good president—and the president himself kept repeating that he had important work to do and would not be diverted from it. Most people accepted the pro-Clinton frame and rejected the Clinton-hating claim. And for good reason. Most White Houses—or for that matter, most corporate boardrooms, most newsrooms and most churches—have had their share of adulterous relationships. So people concluded that the decision point was whether this talented president should be removed from his job because of his personal misconduct.

(One quick note: Paul knew Clinton was going to survive this when, in the early days of the scandal, he was sitting at Mass and the Irish priest told this story: "A man came into the confessional and confessed a sin of a marital nature. So the priest says to him, 'You've cheated on your wife? Obviously, you've got to resign your job.'" After a brief, uncomfortable pause, the congregation started laughing. Then the priest delivered the punch line: "Now, wouldn't that be the dumbest thing you've ever heard? The one has nothing to do with the other." Once a priest had framed the debate that way, Paul felt certain most Americans would do the same. Most Washington pundits, on the other hand, had framed the issue quite differently. They were sure Clinton was through and remain puzzled to this day about how they could have been so wrong. Just goes to show you that people—especially priests—are smarter than pundits.)

Controlling the Agenda

In politics today there is a titanic struggle going on over what's known as agenda setting. On one side are politicians who believe that they should decide what their campaigns will be based on, and if the voters don't like the issues they've chosen to run on, they won't win. Besides, the politicians argue, they're in touch with the voters. They're the ones who go door to door, neighborhood to neighborhood. They're the ones who survey public opinion through polls, focus groups, town-hall meetings and constituent mailings. So they're the best suited to determine the issues on which they'll conduct their campaign.

Sounds sensible, doesn't it?

On the other side is the media. A new and interesting school of journalism, called civic journalism, asserts that too many difficult issues are ignored during campaigns. So they do their own polls and focus groups. They conduct their own town-hall meetings. And they press the politicians to address the issues the journalists believe the election should be about. And if the politicians won't do so, they'll write a story in the paper that says Politician X won't take a stand on Important Issue Y.

That sounds sensible, too, doesn't it?

That's why it's such a hot debate.

It's not merely an academic debate, either. The issues that dominate an election become the issues that office-holders are obliged to deal with. Politicians know this, and the smart ones use their campaigns as referenda on their issue agenda so that if they win, they can argue that they have a mandate to enact their policy proposals.

We tend to side with the politicians. If a candidate wants to run a single-issue campaign on, say, taking the sugar out of cereals, isn't that her prerogative?

I'm Emily Kretchner, candidate for governor. If I'm elected, I will do everything in my power to attack the number one issue facing our state: too much sugar in our breakfast cereals. As a mother, I've seen my own children so hopped up on Sugar Pops, they were bouncing off the walls. Then they get to school and they're too wired to work. They wind up disrupting the class, making smart-aleck comments to the teacher and getting into fights during recess. Then, when the sugar rush wears off, they're lazy and lethargic. Sugar-filled cereals are screwing up our test scores, contributing to the dropout rate and leading our children on a frenzied rush to a life of crime. Make me your governor and Cap'n Crunch will go down with his ship.

You can almost hear the smart guys in the editorial rooms revving up their word processors to take her apart.

Without so much as a word about abortion, the environment, taxes, crime or welfare, Ms. Kretchner seeks our state's highest office. A jeremiad against processed sugar is ludicrous. The food manufacturers and the FDA assure us the cereals are perfectly healthy. Ms. Kretchner would do well to broaden her horizons, abandon her Don Quixote quest against Count Chocula and address the real issues facing this state.

But our heroine Emily sees things differently:

You want to fight crime? Stop sending kids into the world wired on Cocoa Puffs. You want to reduce welfare dependency? Help low-income families afford brain food like wheat germ. Abortion? There'd be a lot fewer unwanted pregnancies if teenagers' brains weren't scrambled by all that sugar. And the environment? The crap we pour into our unsuspecting kids' cereal bowls each morning contains as many toxins as a Superfund site. The reason the newspaper is attacking my candidacy is because it's in the pocket of the grocery stores. Safeway and Piggly Wiggly are its largest advertisers, and sugar-filled cereals are among their most profitable products. And my opponent? He, too, is in the pocket of Tony the Tiger. I'm being attacked because I'm the lone candidate with the courage to speak the truth.

Emily's message is likely to be seen as eccentric at best, irrelevant at worst. But even a bad message is better than no message at all. What if her opponent tries to feed the voters the standard, contentless pabulum so many of the current crop of blow-dried politicians are dishing up these days? Something like this:

I'm Dirk Dolittle. I'm running for governor because I truly love this state. I was born here. My lovely wife, Louise, and I have raised three wonderful children here. If you love our state as much as we do, if you want us to have a future as bright as the best days of our proud past, I'd appreciate your support.

Dirk is full of more crap than a Christmas goose.

And he's not presenting a clear choice. Heck, he isn't presenting a choice at all. Assuming Emily loves the state as much as Dirk does, it doesn't look like Dirk has offered any distinction upon which a voter could choose to prefer him.

Emily's objective is clear: to win the election. Her strategy is to run a single-issue campaign. As political strategists, our hearts are with Emily. A candidate ought to have the right to run her campaign on any issue or issues she chooses. If she doesn't focus on the issues that are most important to the voters, the marketplace theory of politics says her opponent will—and she'll lose.

But as citizens who believe we need to force politicians to face tough issues, we sympathize with the press, too. Candidates who run issueless campaigns, and win, usually fail once in office.

Ronald Reagan and Bill Clinton, on the other hand, ran issue-based campaigns. So when they won, they took their mandate to Congress and got most of it enacted. That's why they were both reelected and are considered to be the most successful politicians of the post-Vietnam era.

Reagan and Clinton knew that the key to their victory— both as candidates and as presidents—was to frame the debate. It's the key to your victory, too. He who defines the debate wins the debate.

Miz Nippy and the Bass Boat

While it's most noticeable in a political campaign or a war with the press, struggles over framing a decision take place in business every day. James's late mama, Miz Nippy Carville, was the queen of framing a debate. She put her eight children through college by selling encyclopedias door to door in and around her home of Carville, Louisiana.

Framing the decision was central to her sales pitch. She'd patrol a neighborhood looking for two telltale signs that a family was a good prospect: children's toys and a bass boat. Being perhaps the most Catholic state in the union, and calling itself "The Sportsmen's Paradise," Louisiana has an inordinate number of homes with both. She'd go to the door—preferably in the evening or on the weekend—and ask to see the man of the house. Now, conventional wisdom has it that women are a softer touch for children's books, but Miz Nippy knew more than the conventional wisdom. She knew how to frame the choice in a way that would shame the customer.

We wish you could've seen her. "You the father of these children?" she'd ask. When the daddy would grunt his assent, she'd start laying it on thick (see Rule Two). "Such beautiful children," she'd gush. Then she'd exchange a word or two with one of the kids and, feigning shock the likes of which would have made Scarlett O'Hara proud, she'd say, "And so bright! My, sir, these children are indeed gifted. They have such potential. You must spend a lot of time with them, reading the encyclopedia. You *do* have a set of encyclopedias, don't you?"

When the guy said they didn't, his goose was cooked.

"Why, sir, how can that be? Such potential in these children, such God-given talent, and you're going to let it go to waste? Surely not. I am going to personally arrange for you to purchase one of the finest collections of children's educational materials ever published."

If the man said he didn't want it or, worse, couldn't afford it, Miz Nippy sprang the trap: "I see you can afford that beautiful bass boat, can't you? You can't tell me that chasing a bunch of pea-brained bass around a bayou is more important to you than the future of your children! You don't want them to grow up ignorant, do you? Trapped in a dead-end job, or unable to get a job at all, just because you and your beer buddies thought fishing was a more important thing to spend your money on than your children's education and their future?"

About that time the guy would look down sheepishly at the half-empty, now-warm bottle of beer in his hand. Then he'd gaze at his bass boat, which until that moment had been such a source of pride, such an unalloyed joy. Now, all of a sudden, it was a source of shame. And he was hooked better than any bass ever was.

The poor bastard never really stood a chance.

Once Miz Nippy framed the debate, the decision was a forgone conclusion. The battle was over before it had begun.

In every decision, that struggle takes place. Sometimes it's overt and sometimes it's unnoticed. Notice it. Engage it. Define the decision point and frame it in the light most favorable to you and you'll win more often than you'll lose.

A Tug of War over Framing the Debate

At the beginning of the Monica Lewinsky scandal, Tim Russert invited Paul on *Meet the Press*. At the time Paul was one of the top officials of the Clinton White House. But Clinton chose not to confide in Paul the truth of his relationship with Lewinsky.

Paul knew that Russert wanted him on *Meet* to talk about the very issue on which Clinton had kept him in the dark. But Paul went on the show anyway. He had a goal of his own: to complain about what he believed was the heavy-handed tactics of special prosecutor Ken Starr.

That interview is a classic tug-of-war over framing the debate. Like the good journalist that he is, Russert tried to corner Paul about the true nature of Clinton's relationship with Lewinsky. And Paul was just as determined to decry publicly what he found to be thuggish tactics by Starr.

Here's what happened. Look at how many times Russert returns to the same question. And look at how many times Paul returns to the same answer—not the answer Russert wants to hear, but the answer Paul wants to give.

RUSSERT: A very simple question: What was the relationship between President Clinton and Monica Lewinsky?

BEGALA: Well, what it is, it's a subject of an ongoing investigation. Because of that, people like me are not free to insert ourselves into that investigation, nor are those conducting the investigation free to leak. And what we have seen is an ongoing campaign of leaks and lies that, frankly, I think have a political ax to grind and are worthy of an investigation. Members of Congress have called for this. Thoughtful commentators have called for it. And I think it's time to investigate the investigators to see where these leaks are coming from.

RUSSERT: Why won't the president of the United States come forward and say to the American people, "This is what happened. This is why she visited the White House thirty-seven times. This is why she sent me six gifts. This is why she had a job at the White House, the Pentagon, and a job offer at the UN. This is why I gave her gifts." . . . We get nothing from the White House. Zippo.

BEGALA: Because it is the subject of an investigation that itself has dragged its heels for four years now. And, frankly, if we had confidence that the independent counsel was truly independent, that the investigation was truly fair, you might have a different story. But let me give you a couple of specifics. You know this: Ken Starr makes over $1 million a year from tobacco money, some of the most bitter political opponents the president has had. At least four witnesses have come forward and said that Starr and his office have tried to intimidate them into changing their testimony and testifying falsely. . . . So there are a lot of questions about this investigation, and sound lawyers have laid down the law for the president and said, "You cannot, in this atmosphere, with this kind of a partisan investigation, with the power unchecked that this prosecutor has, subject yourself to this."

RUSSERT: But this is the White House defense: Change the subject.

BEGALA: No, no. It is the subject.

RUSSERT: Attack Ken Starr. Attack the media. Let me go back to the issue before us, that why won't the president of the United States come forward and talk about this candidly? He is not bound by any law, any regulation, any court order. The only reason he won't is because—you just said it—he may put himself in legal jeopardy.

BEGALA: Because we have seen an ongoing campaign—let me tell you, it's not just the White House. Ms. Lewinsky's counsel told the Associated Press, and I quote, "The office of independent counsel is conducting an orchestrated campaign to pressure Ms. Lewinsky into statements that are not true." There's a professor of law at the University of Arkansas who claims he was threatened, intimidated. They said they were going to investigate his mother if he didn't sign a statement that was false.

RUSSERT: Again, let me . . . we'll get to Ken Starr.

BEGALA: And I could go on and on about witnesses who have been squeezed. If he . . . this is why—

RUSSERT: We'll get to Ken Starr, but let me go back to the president. Three weeks ago, "You'll get your answers."

BEGALA: Absolutely.

RUSSERT: "Legitimate questions. We'll get to them quickly."

BEGALA: Right.

RUSSERT: Nothing.

BEGALA: Because this investigation is grinding on. He cannot comment on this for good reasons that his lawyers have articulated.

RUSSERT: What are the reasons? What good reasons?

BEGALA: Because, as I've said very candidly—probably more candidly than the lawyers would want me to—that there are real questions about this investigation. I believe, Tim, that Ken Starr has become corrupt in the sense that Lord Acton meant when he said "Absolute power corrupts absolutely."

RUSSERT: We now understand that Betty Currie turned over to Kenneth Starr gifts that the president had given to Monica Lewinsky.

BEGALA: I have no idea if that's true because of these leaks.

RUSSERT: But where did she get them from?

BEGALA: Where did these leaks come from?

RUSSERT: Why won't the president—

BEGALA: I can't confirm that or I'm participating in these leaks. Let me ask you real quickly—

RUSSERT: But the president . . . wait a minute. The president promised the most ethical administration in history.

BEGALA: Absolutely.

RUSSERT: Why won't he come forward and level with the American people? I ask you—

BEGALA: He has. He said these are false charges, and a fair investigation will prove that. Now, part of the reason this investigation is not fair is because of the leaks. And I need to ask you, has NBC News been the recipient of illegal leaks from Ken Starr?

RUSSERT: We don't talk about whether leaks come from the White House, from Ken Starr, from the State Department, from the Pentagon. We do our job and we do it well.

. . . .

RUSSERT: Well, Mr. Begala, let's get beyond the leaks, let's get beyond Ken Starr—

BEGALA: I wish we could.

RUSSERT: —all the speculation. Only one person can come forward and say to the American people, "This is what happened."

BEGALA: Absolutely.

RUSSERT: One more time, why does the president refuse to come before the American people and explain this in its totality?

BEGALA: Because we have a situation here where an investigator is, in the words of many thoughtful critics, "out of control"; where I turn on NBC News and see Claire Shipman, one of the best in the business, respected White House reporter, say, and I quote, "Sources in Starr's office have told NBC News that information Lewinsky's lawyers were offering was simply not enough. Sources in Starr's office believe the instructions came from the White House."

Now, when sources in Starr's office are cited that way, by a solid reporter like Claire Shipman, forgive me for concluding that sources in Starr's office are leaking, and that might be criminal; a much more serious crime, frankly, than signing a false affidavit by a twenty-four-year-old kid in a civil lawsuit.

. . . .

RUSSERT: Finally, as I showed before, the president said three weeks ago we would get answers to legitimate questions quickly. When will the president answer these questions in their totality?

BEGALA: That is much more up to Judge Starr. When we learn about four witnesses who say that they have been intimidated and told to lie, we are troubled.

When we see another witness, as reported in the *New York Observer,* who changed his story after he was be-friended by the head of a slush fund operated by Ken Starr's patron, Richard Mellon Scaife, who set up a $1 million teaching job for Ken Starr to move into in Mal-ibu, California, as soon as he's finished with this in-vestigation.

RUSSERT: So when will we hear from the president?

BEGALA: When the investigation allows him to do so, Tim. But until then his lawyers—

RUSSERT: No, no, there is no—

BEGALA: —have laid down the law.

RUSSERT: There is no rule prohibiting the president now from talking.

BEGALA: There is a sensible rule of common sense that his lawyers have laid down, and I happen to agree with them; that even though politically I'd like to see him put this investigation behind him immediately, when you have an out-of-control investigation on this, when you have this sort of a situation, it is best to listen to your lawyers and to do what is best for the American people, which is focus on your job, not to spend all of his time commenting on every leak and every lie coming out of Ken Starr.

RUSSERT: That has to be the last word, Paul Begala. To be continued.[1]

At least a dozen times in that interview, Russert asked Paul why Clinton wouldn't simply tell the American people the true nature of his relationship with Monica Lewinsky. And at least as many times Paul responded by decrying the tactics of the Starr operation. Afterward, the interview made a front-page, above-the-fold story in *The New York Times*. Tim later told Paul, "We both did our jobs."

When George W. Bush was planning to run for president, his media adviser told Paul he'd used a tape of that interview to help train Bush on how to stay on the message in the face of hostile questions. While we're not fans of Junior's, it is undeniably true that he learned that message well. Bush is a relentlessly focused messenger. And that skill is one of the biggest reasons he is where he is today.

Understand the Difference Between Strategy and Tactics

THE United States Military Academy teaches its cadets to analyze a mission on three tiers: Objective, Strategy and Tactics.

The objective is the broad goal. Strategy is the plan of action for achieving the goal. And tactics are the various steps you take to get there.

Take D Day, for example. The objective was to save the world and defeat Nazi tyranny. The strategy was to open up an eastern front against Hitler in Europe. The tactic was a feint to Calais, then an amphibious landing, supported by paratroopers, at Normandy.

Articulating the objective is usually the easiest part. In a campaign it's winning the White House—or the Governor's Mansion or the Senate seat or whatever. It's a big, broad goal so obvious that it almost doesn't have to be stated. But it's worth stating—and keeping in mind. Too many people, businesses, sports teams and politicians define their objective too low. How many times have we heard a coach tell a sports reporter, "Next year we're going to the Super Bowl"? He's usually the coach who goes to the Super Bowl—and then loses. Going to the Super Bowl is not the objective. Winning the damn Super Bowl is the objective.

Same with campaigns. Many campaigns are two-stage events: first a primary, then a general election. The primary, since it's within a party, tends to be ideological and nasty. And in the heat of battle candidates often lose sight of the fact that the objective is to win the general election.

Thus Al Gore was so hot to defeat Bill Bradley in the 2000 primaries that he tacked too far to the left, calling for registration and licensing of handguns, saying he'd institute a gays-in-the-military litmus test for his chairman of the Joint Chiefs of Staff, railing about the Confederate battle flag. These liberal positions made him popular among the true believers in the Democratic primaries, but they went a long way toward alienating the swing voters in the swing states that were to decide the general election. Cultural conservatives in states like North Carolina, Georgia, Kentucky, West Virginia, Arkansas and even Gore's home state of Tennessee had supported Clinton in the past, but they abandoned Gore in 2000. That's what happens when you lose sight of your objective.

The pattern continued throughout the Gore campaign. From pandering to right-wing Cuban-Americans over Elian Gonzalez to flip-flopping over the Strategic Petroleum Reserve, Gore forever looked like . . . well, like Bush said he looked like: a man who would say or do anything to become president.

Gore never had a strategy for dealing with President Clinton or the adultery scandal. On the day Clinton was impeached, Gore said he was "a man I believe will be regarded in the history books as one of our greatest presidents." We happen to believe that's true, but in retrospect a lot of voters probably thought Gore was only saying that because Clinton's popularity was near an all-time high.

Six months later, on his announcement day, Gore had a new tactic: He expressed shock and disappointment that Clinton had had the affair. Truth be told, either reaction is defensible; be a diehard Clinton defender or be a disillusioned, disgusted former friend. But don't switch from one to the other depending on the transitory politics of the day. That's tactical. And tactics without a strategy is nothing more than spitting in the wind.

Clinton in 1992 did not lack strategic focus. Even as his primary campaign was teetering on the brink of oblivion, he kept uppermost in his mind that the real goal was to unseat Bush the elder and win the White House. That focus helped to keep him calm in the storm and allowed him to win the nomination and unite his party.

So set your goals high. But that's just the beginning. After that, you've got to devise a strategy for achieving your goal. Then—and only then—you can set about deciding which tactics will get you there.

If some campaigns founder because of lack of clear objectives, even more of them confuse strategy with tactics. Strategy is hard. Tactics are easy. In 1992 Clinton's basic strategy did not change from the beginning of the primary to the end of the general election. It was first to win the Democratic Party's presidential nomination as the candidate of change: a new-ideas New Democrat who could fix the economy, then defeat Bush in the general election as . . .

well . . . the candidate of change; a new-ideas New Democrat who could fix the economy. We had our share of tactical tacks back and forth, but Clinton never lost sight of the objective (winning the White House) or the strategy (new ideas for the economy).

Our staff, however, was frequently distracted. That's why James put up a sign in the War Room. A sign that quickly became famous. What it actually said was:

> CHANGE VERSUS MORE OF THE SAME
> IT'S THE ECONOMY, STUPID
> AND DON'T FORGET HEALTH CARE

Change was the message, and positioning Clinton as the candidate of change was the strategy. The economy, health care, welfare, reinventing government and all the rest were illustrations of that basic message; they were tactics, not strategy. Without the overarching theme of economic change for the middle class, Clinton would have looked like one more opportunistic politician who promised everything to everybody. The kind of guy who, if he were speaking to a group of cannibals, would promise them missionaries.

Executing a Strategy Requires Constant Focus

In our years as political consultants, there were many times when people would ask us to come in and assess an ailing campaign. We'd go to the headquarters, walk around, talk to people, ask them what was going on—and what was going wrong. Of course, asking someone what's wrong with a losing political campaign is a little like asking a rodeo bull rider where it hurts. He's going to say, "Everywhere." If a campaign is failing, it's usually systemic. So we'd get a lot of input.

One guy would tell us, "You know, when people call in they never know what they're going to get. Sometimes it's 'Jones for Senate,' sometimes it's 'Jones Campaign,' sometimes it's 'Jones 2000.' There's no consistency in the phone answering."

Okay. Then we'd move on to the next person.

"I'll tell you what's wrong with this campaign. The volunteers come in and they don't have the right kind of assignment. We've got people with high-tech backgrounds licking stamps and people with bad eyesight hammering nails into yard signs. It's a mess."

Fine.

But eventually we'd find someone—usually a young person who was too inexperienced to be full of bad habits and myopic observations. And he or she would say, "Well, gee, I don't know much. But it seems to me no one in this state knows why they should vote for Jones instead of Smith."

Stop.

That person has a future. The problem isn't how you answer the phone or who's hammering nails into yard signs. The problem is not that the color on the yard signs doesn't match the color on the billboards. The problem is that the people you're trying to reach don't understand what you're trying to say.

So much of the energy of a campaign—or of any other enterprise—goes into the small questions, the "how" questions. Not nearly enough goes into the big, existential questions like "What are we doing?" and "Why are we doing it?" Those questions seem simple. And they are. But simplicity and importance are not mutually exclusive. It's been our experience that those simple questions are the hardest to answer and the easiest to avoid.

Same with campaigns. There are always people who fill up time in meetings with worrying about how the campaign communicates: Do we need television spots or is radio more effective? What colors do we need in the logo? (It's instructive that the Gore campaign bragged that Gore personally designed his campaign's logo, while in response the Bush campaign bragged that Bush didn't care a whit what the logo looked like. Though we voted for Gore, Bush was right on this one.) How important will the Internet be in our communications plan? Do we use billboards or bus benches? (We once actually worked on a campaign in Texas where someone told us that no one in San Antonio pays attention to television—it's bus benches. Nothing matters but having the right bus benches. We always suspected that guy had a brother-in-law in the bus-bench business. Either that or he was a genuine idiot.)

These questions aren't irrelevant, but they're a whole lot less important than *what* you communicate. The coolest logo and the brightest colors can't make up for a weak-ass message.

So why do people waste so much time on tactics that are unimportant compared with the larger strategic questions? Probably for the same reason you've asked yourself "What should I wear?" a lot more often than you've asked "Why am I alive?" Simple questions are the toughest. If you want to be the smartest one in the big meeting, return again and again to the fundamentals. Let someone else whirl around in circles about the details. If you get the big things right, the details are just that: details.

If you as a leader lose sight of your strategic objective for even a single moment, you will be astonished by how quickly everyone under you begins to focus on the most inane, irrelevant, goofy crap imaginable. They've got to focus on something. And if they're not being given a strategic focus from the top, they'll focus on something else. Which will only force you to focus on fixing their mistakes and so on, leading to a death spiral.

You, Too, Can Run a Major Airline

Herb Kelleher, the genius businessman who created Southwest Airlines, once told Paul: "I can teach you the secret to running this airline in thirty seconds. This is it: Southwest is the low-fare airline. Not *a* low-fare airline. We are *THE* low-fare airline. Once you understand that fact, you can make any decision about this company's future as well as I can.

"Here's an example," Herb said. "Tracy from marketing comes into your office. She says her surveys indicate that the passengers might enjoy a light entrée on the Houston to Las Vegas flight. All we offer is peanuts, and she thinks a nice chicken Caesar salad would be popular. What do you say?"

Paul stammered. So Herb told him: "You say, 'Tracy, will adding that chicken Caesar salad make us *THE* low-fare airline from Houston to Las Vegas? Because if it doesn't help us become the unchallenged low-fare airline, we're not serving any damn chicken salad.' "

Focus on strategy. Maybe Tracy's chicken Caesar salad would have moved the needle on customer satisfaction. But that's a tactic. Herb Kelleher did not want Southwest to be the most comfortable airline or the airline with the best-fed passengers. His strategy was to be the low-cost airline. And his every decision—from building a fleet of nothing but 737s (reduces maintenance costs and allows every pilot, mechanic and flight attendant to become an expert on the aircraft without having to know about seven variations for seven different planes), to which airports to serve (only those whose landing fees are not astronomical)—was a part of that strategy.

Focus on strategy. In the words of the old spiritual that became an anthem for the civil rights movement: "Keep Your Eyes on the Prize." Herb never took his eyes off the prize. Where a less farsighted businessman might have tried to keep costs down by treating his employees like dirt, Herb understood that speed (in this case, quick turnarounds at the gate), safety and flexibility would do more to keep costs down than screwing his employees. So Southwest has the most heavily unionized workforce in the airline business— and the happiest. Because Herb had a strategy and he imbued that strategy in the heart of every person who worked for him. And they executed that strategy.

Newt's Law of Field Mice and Antelope

Newt Gingrich is one of the most successful political leaders of our time. Yes, we disagreed with virtually everything he did, but this is a book about strategy, not ideology. And we've got to give Newt his due. His strategic ability—his relentless focus on capturing the House of Representatives for the Republicans—led to one of the biggest political landslides in American history.

Now that he's in the private sector, Newt uses a brilliant illustration to explain the need to focus on the big things and let the little stuff slide: the analogy of the field mice and the antelope.

A lion is fully capable of capturing, killing and eating a field mouse. But it turns out that the energy required to do so exceeds the caloric content of the mouse itself. So a lion that spent its day hunting and eating field mice would slowly starve to death. A lion can't live on field mice. A lion needs antelope.

Antelope are big animals. They take more speed and strength to capture and kill, and once killed, they provide a feast for the lion and her pride. A lion can live a long and happy life on a diet of antelope.

The distinction is important. Are you spending all your time and exhausting all your energy catching field mice? In the short term it might give you a nice, rewarding feeling. But in the long run you're going to die. So ask yourself at the end of the day, "Did I spend today chasing mice or hunting antelope?" If you're honest with yourself and the answer is mice, you'd better reassess your focus, get back to the strategic core and get your butt on the trail of an antelope.

At the beginning of President Clinton's first term he spent his time hunting mice, antelope, armadillos and dachshunds—anything and everything that moved. His physical and intellectual energies were nearly limitless, and when you're president, the world truly is your oyster. If you want to know everything there is to know about the wool and mohair subsidy, the Assistant Deputy Administrator for Wool and the Vice-Under-Secretary for Mohair will be in the Oval Office in five minutes. At the same time, Clinton was trying to focus on a few big things: his economic plan, his health care plan and his crime plan. But the mice-hunting was exhausting even him.

Unlike the stereotype of a politician who's an empty vessel into which advisers pour content, Clinton's cup runneth over. He was so insatiably interested in everything—and he came from a state with fewer than two and a half million people, where he pretty much could focus on every problem.

To his credit, he reassessed, streamlined and began distinguishing between field mice and antelope. He learned to empower and delegate and stop micromanaging. His senior staff got used to telling him, "No, sir. That issue isn't ready for your attention yet. We're still working on it at the staff level." That left him with enough time to think, read and focus on the big things, like how to deal with the bombing of the Murrah Federal Building in Oklahoma City in 1995, or the Kosovo war of 1999. We believe one of the great keys to the Clinton comeback was his ability to maintain a strategic rather than a tactical focus.

The Tactical Retreat

People think that spin is lying. If that was true, anyone could do it, and we wouldn't be paid the kind of money we're paid. Far from lying, spin—effective, credible, successful spin—requires a gut level of honesty.

Truly effective spin—and any truly effective strategy—must have room for a tactical retreat. Not a full-fledged, turn-tail-and-run kind of retreat. But a tactical retreat, which allows you to regroup, gather strength and mount a new offensive.

In an argument a tactical retreat buys you something very precious: credibility. When you see a spin doctor on TV give a little ground, you immediately think, "Well, at least she's being honest about the downside of her position." But when someone refuses to give an inch, rather than admire his steadfastness, we usually see him as a pigheaded horse's ass. (This raises the troubling question of whether a horse's ass can have a pig's head. That would require either a revival of the old vaudeville pantomime animals, mixed and matched, or a truly bold high-tech experiment in cross-species genetic engineering. But we digress.)

Our favorite tactical retreat—one that built credibility, refocused the debate and allowed his side to march to victory—came in that great film classic *Animal House*. When the hated Dean Wormer calls the boys from Delta House before the crypto-fascist Interfraternity Council to railroad them off campus for having too much fun, one of Delta House's leaders, Chip "Otter" Stratton, makes his stand: "Ladies and gentlemen, I'll be brief. The issue here is not whether we broke a few rules or took a few liberties with our female party guests. We did."

Instead of advancing the preposterous argument that the residents of Animal House were choirboys, Otter acknowledges reality. And when he talks about taking "a few liberties with our female party guests" he winks at Dean Wormer, whose wife was one of those party guests. You gotta admire his mix of candor and *cojones*.

But having made his tactical retreat, Otter proceeds to make his strategic advance. He redefines the debate (see Rule Four): "But you can't hold a whole fraternity responsible for the behavior of a few sick, perverted individuals. For if you do, then shouldn't we blame the whole fraternity system? And if the whole fraternity system is guilty, then isn't this an indictment of our educational institutions in general?"

Then, turning to the Hitler Youth chairman of the Interfraternity Council, Greg Marmalard, Otter makes this challenge: "I put it to you, Greg. Isn't this an indictment of our entire American society? Well, you can do what you want to us, but we're not going to sit here and listen to you badmouth the United States of America!"

And with that burst of bravado he leads the "gentlemen"

of Delta House out of the kangaroo court, as they hum "The Star-Spangled Banner."

Otter understood strategy. Let's be clear. We're not recommending that you create a car-size cake with "Eat Me" written on it and drive it in the big parade as they did in *Animal House*. We're saying that you have to think on several levels at once. Far too many people fail because they are good tacticians but lousy strategists. They can get through the day, and the next, and the next. But one day they look up and see they're further away from their goal than they were on the day they began.

You have to keep your ultimate objective in mind at all times, design a multistep strategy for getting there and then—within that strategy and in pursuit of that objective—have the flexibility to tack one way or another as circumstances dictate moment by moment.

Be Open

ONE of the dirty little secrets of life is that there are damn few real secrets in life. Or at least damn few secrets worth expending a lot of your energy to keep secret.

This rule is a big one with us. People who sneak around, rely on subterfuge and deceit, people who don't say what they mean and don't mean what they say, folks who always have a hidden agenda—they may think of themselves as Machiavellian. But with all due respect to Niccolò Machiavelli, we think of them as enormous pains in the ass.

There's no doubt that there's much wisdom in *The Prince*. And while misdirection has its place, it is more a tactic than a strategy. And if you make it a way of life, you're not a strategist. You're just a liar.

When James wrote his book about Ken Starr, he was up-front from the get-go. He began the book by saying, "You know something? I don't like Ken Starr." And when Paul wrote his book about Bush, there was no beating around the . . . well . . . you get the point. Some folks hated what we had to say and other folks loved our little treatises.

But no one could accuse us of having hidden agendas. We believe that being up-front with people confers respect. It pays them the compliment of candor. Even if you're delivering bad news—or in our case a political screed—chances are most folks who disagree with you will respect you if you put your cards on the table.

So don't be a sneaky little shit.

Too many people confuse secrecy with importance. "Oh, this is a big deal, let's not tell anybody about it." And, to be sure, some things really *are* secret: patents or trade secrets or hostage negotiations or launch codes for nukes. But contrast that list with all the crap that the government and business and campaigns keep secret, and think about all that wasted energy.

Maybe our view is colored by the fact that we work in politics, where there really are no secrets. Everything in Washington leaks. Every president in the media age has been driven to distraction by leaks. Nixon went so far as to bug his own staffers, wiretap reporters and call for the firebombing of the Brookings Institution. He'd have been better off if he'd just gone bowling. The president of the United States of America is the most powerful person in the history of the world. With a word he can rain death and destruction down on faraway places. He can spend a trillion dollars with the stroke of his pen. He can, literally, blow up the world. But he can't stop leaks.

In the information age, trying to hoard and control information is like peeing in the wind. You can try it, but you're just going to wind up unhappy, uncomfortable and smelly. Openness, or what the international business folks call "transparency," is the way of the future.

The War Room was open—literally, it was a big, open room. But it was also open culturally. James used to tell the folks who worked there, "We're not a secretive organization. We have a philosophy. We have a message. We're trying to tell 280 million people what we're about. We're in the information-dissemination business. We're not in the information-hoarding business."

Hell, we were so open we let movie cameras come in. And if you think anyone was preening for the cameras, think again. We had one focus: to win. If we didn't win that race, there wouldn't have been a movie called *The War Room*. It would've been called *Loser Central*.

By the way, openness makes it easier to keep the secrets you really need to keep. Huh? Here's how. First, your organization isn't required to expend so much energy on keeping little chickenshit things secret that they let the big secret out of the bag. Second, the bigger deal you make about a secret, the more likely it is to leak.

Just Say It

This is especially important if your function is to communicate something to voters or consumers or customers or investors. You can be so consumed with keeping things to yourself that no one ever finds out what it is you're trying to communicate in the first place.

When James was starting out in the political consulting business, he once made a television ad for a candidate. It was utterly indecipherable. Thirty seconds of the most confusing, unfocused B.S. you ever saw. And when it came time for James to show it to his boss at the consulting firm—as well as to the candidate—he punched Play and let 'er rip.

When the spot was finished, the candidate seemed confused. He asked, "Would you play that over again?" So

James proudly played it again. "You know," the candidate said, "I'm not sure I know what the heck that spot's about."

And the head of the firm, who didn't want to embarrass James, burst out with this gem: "Do you want the opposition to know?"

And you can rest assured that the opposition had no idea what that spot said. Then, again, neither did the voters. James (not to mention his candidate) would have been a lot better off with an ad that had no obuse angles but rather went straight to the point. Being open also means being direct.

Openness Empowers People

As a leader, including the people you work with in the information loop empowers them. It's conceivable that if you have a completely autocratic structure, it is actually possible to order people to do something without telling them where it fits into what everyone else is doing and without telling them why they should do it. It's a safe bet that Osama bin Laden doesn't spend a lot of time buying his lunatic terrorist droids into every detail of his latest cowardly attack. But you didn't buy this book to get leadership tips from Osama bin Laden.

For one thing, you've got to spend all of your time making sure they do it right—because if people don't understand how their piece fits into the bigger picture and don't understand the rationale behind the order they've been given, they're more likely to screw it up.

It's a funny thing about human nature. We generally do better work when we know what the hell we're doing and why the hell we're doing it. And if you give people the authority to think for themselves, they just might think of things you didn't. That thought must surely horrify the anal-retentive control freaks out there, but it's true.

Erskine Bowles is a successful businessman who served for a time as President Clinton's White House chief of staff. As Counselor to the President, Paul was one of the top aides on the White House staff, and his job involved coordinating policy and politics. He once went to Bowles with a question that was in essence a political call. Erskine told him to decide it for himself. "I don't believe in buying a dog and then doin' my own barking" were his exact words. (Erskine's from North Carolina, where they talk like that. Had he been a New Yorker he might have said "Fuhgetaboutit.")

Successful campaigns place a premium on creativity, initiative and action. But people can't think for themselves if they don't have the information on which to base a decision. You can't delegate authority and then hoard information.

In the War Room we didn't even keep our polls under lock and key. They were our most sensitive internal information, the one thing we wouldn't want in the papers, and yet more often than not they could be found lying on James's desk. Stan Greenberg, our pollster, would discuss the latest data with James in the middle of the War Room, which, remember, was a wide-open place.

And you know what? We never once had a poll leak. Never. We trusted people with information. We treated people as if they were responsible, indispensable parts of an important enterprise. And they acted like it.

That kind of openness—and the empowerment it represents—should go up and down the line in an organization. By being open with information, especially with our strategic goals, we empowered relatively junior people to make some of the most important decisions of the campaign. A group of young turks called the Overnight Crew staffed the War Room during the night. They collected news from every key target area, digested it and presented it to the rest of the team at the 7:30 A.M. meeting. The decisions those folks made—what to report and what not to report—formed the basis for every tactical decision we made. Reporting from all fifty states and Washington, D.C., would have been too unwieldy. Somebody had to separate the important from the minutiae—at 4:00 or 5:00 or 6:00 in the morning—so that by 7:30 they could answer the important questions: Is Bush visiting Michigan? Does Perot have a new anti-Clinton ad on TV in Oregon? Did an influential columnist in Georgia just trash us? Because our overnight team was fully aware of our polling and our strategy, they had the ability to make good decisions. And we had the ability to sleep through the night.

The Lack of Openness Breeds Mistrust

Earlier in this book we told the story of how *The New York Times* blew the initial take on Whitewater. (See Rule Three.) In fairness to the *Times* (which wasn't always fair to the Clintons, but what the hell, this book isn't about score settling), the Clintons didn't help the paper. New to the national limelight, where everyone who wants to serve is immediately presumed to be a crook, the Clintons naively thought that if someone was accusing them of wrongdoing, the best thing to do would be to call a lawyer. Besides, this was a long-ago business deal, not a political issue. So they asked an attorney to deal with the *Times* story.

Big mistake.

Lawyers are trained to admit nothing, to give no ground.

Political pros know that credibility comes from having a little give in your position—and most of all it comes from being open. It was a classic clash of cultures: the *Times* believed it had the public's best interests at heart, ferreting out a story that looked to them like a sweetheart deal between a powerful politician and a businessman. The Clintons' lawyer thought she had her clients' best interests at heart by revealing nothing. But stonewalling is the biggest, brightest red flag you can wave at a reporter. And *The New York Times* is the biggest, strongest, meanest bull in the corral. No wonder it charged.

If political pros, used to handling the press, had dealt with that original story, would things have been different? Hard to say. The Clintons did have some extraordinarily dedicated adversaries who proved adept at leading a remarkably gullible national press corps around by the nose. But we do know this: holding back information from the *Times* made it harder for the paper to get the facts right the first time. And if you're not helping the press figure out the story, you can rest assured that your adversaries are.

If There's Something Bad to Be Said About You, Say It Yourself

Alice Roosevelt Longworth was the daughter of a president (Teddy Roosevelt), the wife of the Speaker of the House and one of the great legends of Washington society. She is most famous for having said, "If you don't have something nice to say about someone, come sit here by me."

Like most human beings, ol' Alice loved the dirt. And there's something especially delicious about getting it on the sly. Think of the difference when you hear bad news from a third party or from the person himself (or herself):

THIRD PARTY: Did you hear that Raul and Sally are splitting up? Yeah. I hear he was nailing a young woman at the office.

YOU: Cool.

Now take the same facts but get them from the person involved.

RAUL: I'm afraid Sally and I are through. I made a fool of myself with a young woman at the office and she says she can't trust me anymore.

YOU: The young woman at the office can't trust you?

Raul: No, you moron. Sally. We're through.

YOU: I feel so bad for you, Raul.

Hearing the bad news about someone from a third party often elicits schadenfreude, that wonderful German word that means taking pleasure in someone else's pain. But when you hear it from the person directly, there's a lot less schadenfreude and a lot more sympathy.

This is why the press and the political people around Clinton were always pressing to release more information—even damaging information—during the many (mostly trumped-up) investigations of the president. We reasoned that Starr and his band of merry men would leak the most damning stuff in the most negative light possible, so why not tell our side while releasing the bad news ourselves?

Our efforts were complicated by the hybrid political-legal nature of the investigations. The president's lawyers—doing their job—argued that no sensible lawyer would allow his or her client to admit to anything, much less release damaging information about himself in the middle of an investigation. The problem is, we were both right. So we muddled along in the middle, often releasing information before Clinton's adversaries could twist it for their own purposes but also often refusing to release information because there was a legal as well as a political strategy. (For a full discussion on why we believe Clinton's lying about his affair with Monica Lewinsky was a major mistake, turn to Rule Eleven: Know How to Recover When You *Really* Screw Up.)

Being open is not only the right thing to do, it's the smart thing to do. In the information age people are going to catch you in a lie—especially a public lie. (There's still probably a lot of mileage in those small private lies like "Gee, Mom, this chili is great" when, in fact, it's barely edible.) Candor breeds a sense of trust and empowerment. Playing Hide the Ball only breeds distrust and disillusionment. Nobody wants to be treated like the proverbial mushroom—kept in the dark and fed nothing but shit.

Being Open Can Save You—Even After You've Been . . . Well . . . Not So Open

One of the most amazing experiences of our political careers turned on the issue of openness. Zell Miller, our candidate for governor of Georgia in 1990, had performed stunningly well in the statewide-televised debate against his GOP opponent. There had been one rather tense exchange that Miller knocked out of the park. He was asked about a comment he allegedly made back in 1964—a racist attack on Lyndon Johnson when LBJ had gone to Georgia to campaign for Miller's opponent. The reporter questioning Miller in the debate said that Miller had slammed Johnson for supporting civil rights, accusing him of "selling his southern heritage for a mess of dark potage."

As racist comments go, that was hardly the worst we'd ever heard. And it was allegedly made a quarter-century ago. Still, watching the debate, we were stunned. Miller had been one of the leading lights of racial progress in Georgia for decades; he was one of the few white Georgia politicians to endorse civil rights hero John Lewis when he ran for Congress. This hurt.

So we were thrilled when Miller wheeled on his accuser and said that back in 1964 when the *Atlanta Constitution* had printed that so-called quote he'd marched down to the paper's offices and demanded and received a correction. He'd never say a thing like that. A great moment.

The next day that great moment became one of our greatest nightmares. Al May, the veteran political reporter for the *Atlanta Constitution,* interviewed Miller as Paul drove them and Shirley Miller to an event in rural Georgia. May made small talk for a little while. Then he sprang his trap. "Zell," he said, "I've talked to all the editors who were around back then, checked the morgue and the archives, and you never asked for a retraction and the paper never printed one."

"I know," Miller said, biting off the words like they were bitter herbs.

"So why'd you say all that in the debate last night?"

Miller leaned in close to May and said, "Because, Al, I was trying to mislead the people of Georgia."

For one terrible moment Paul thought about wrecking the car. The only thing that stopped him was that Shirley Miller, one of the world's great ladies, was with them. Otherwise he would have gladly rolled the car into the ditch alongside that country road.

Miller opened his heart to May. Told him he'd always been for racial equality but when Lyndon Johnson supported his opponent, he wanted to lash out. He'd regretted that one moment of anger, dressed up as racial division, ever since.

It was as moving, honest and forthcoming a moment as we'd ever seen from a politician. But May had a job to do, and there was no amount of spin, cajoling or threatening that could keep that story out of the paper.

That night we sent a young staffer to the loading dock where the early, Bulldog edition of the *Atlanta Journal-Constitution* rolled out around midnight. Sure enough, there was the headline on the front page of the Metro/State section: "Miller: I Lied."

Uggh.

We went to bed thinking the race might well be over. It's one thing to be thought a liar; it's another to admit it—all in the name of being honest: "Honest, folks, I'm a liar. No, trust me. I'm a liar."

But something happened in the quiet hours between midnight and dawn. For when we awoke and looked at the paper after it hit our doorstep, the headline was gone. The story had been watered down so much that it would barely cause a blip. Apparently, the only edition of the paper that had had the disastrous story was the Bulldog, which had a relatively small press run and was never picked up by Miller's opponent.

To this day we don't know exactly why the paper saved Miller's butt. Our best theory is that the editors decided to give him a break because he'd come so breathtakingly clean. As we wrote this book we thought about calling and asking but decided we didn't want to know. Why argue with divine intervention?

We're not saying that if you're honest—even about lying—that some angel will zoom down from heaven and save you from the consequences of your actions. But it sure worked for Zell Miller.

Rule 7

Know How to Communicate

IF a politician can't get her point across, she'd better find another line of work. A politician who can't communicate is like a mechanic who can't handle a wrench.

We believe that politics is just like real life—only more so.

How many times have we heard about married couples who break up after twenty-five years because they can't communicate? How many friendships have been strained or ended, how many business associations have been fouled up, frayed or finished because of poor communication skills?

Communicating is like anything else. It requires work. We're always amazed at the time and effort business people put into product development, research, engineering, marketing, advertising and all the rest without realizing that the ability to convey information from one person to another, from one department to another, from one division to another, from one company to another is central to the success of all those functions.

When he was prime minister of Great Britain and heading into the election of 1997, John Major appeared on the BBC's *Today* program, the most widely watched morning show in Britain. The legendary journalist Sir David Frost interviewed him, and the only time he seemed particularly energized was when he reflected on modern politics' slavish devotion to the sound bite.

"One of the things I most loathe about politics these days," Major said, "is that it is politics by sound bite. This is a very complex country. The policies to improve it are necessarily complex and difficult. You cannot honestly bring them down to a sound bite without trivializing the debate and misleading the public."

Shortly thereafter Frost also interviewed Major's challenger, Labour's Tony Blair. Same program, same format, same set. But a very different message. When given a similarly open-ended question about the state of British politics, Blair delivered his message with an energy and a vitality that was striking in its contrast to the whiny, self-referential tone Major had set. Blair said the issue was this: "Is Britain the country that it should be? Do we have the society we need? Is our economy really fit to compete in the twenty-first century? Is our political system relevant to the concerns and needs of people today? Now, I think that most British people would say, 'Well, no. We could do a lot better than that.' "

Major went on to suffer one of the worst defeats in British political history. Blair has recently become the first Labour prime minister in British history to win back-to-back victories (and both of them landslides). Why?

A lot of reasons. While the fundamental direction of the

country under the Conservative Party was what ultimately sunk Major, the contrasting styles of the two party leaders also played a role. Look at the two contrasting statements. Major's remark, while itself a sound bite, was nothing more than a whimper about sound bites. It didn't tell a story, didn't relate to anyone's life, didn't offer hope for the future.

Blair, on the other hand, is like his ideological soulmate, Bill Clinton: a brilliant policy wonk who knows how to communicate his ideas effectively in the modern media age. His message was energetic, sharp and focused. More important, the content of his message—improving the economy, modernizing society, updating the political system—was both relevant to the needs and concerns of ordinary Britons and optimistic about the future.

It's easy to wind up like John Major; it's hard to be like Tony Blair. After decades of counseling politicians and businesses on how best to communicate, we've developed five simple rules of great communicating—lessons drawn from political life, which we believe are applicable to your life.

1. TELL A STORY

Facts tell, but stories sell. Human beings process information in the narrative form. That's why, from the Greek myths to the griots of Africa, the history of humanity has been told in stories. If you're not communicating in stories, you're not communicating. You may be presenting a series of facts, many of them perhaps important, but the chances of your audience remembering or being moved by your facts enough to do what you want are nil.

In case you weren't an English major, let's recap the basic elements of the narrative form. A good story has a sympathetic protagonist and an unsympathetic antagonist, a hero and a villain. It has conflict, which creates drama, then resolution. Dudley Do-Right is the hero. Snidely Whiplash is the villain. Little Nell Paulene is the victim. Do-Right and Whiplash clash. The evil Snidely ties Nell to the railroad tracks and—after much tension—Whiplash saves her. She falls into his arms, cooing, "My hero . . ."

Ronald Reagan was the greatest storyteller to grace the White House in the last fifty years. Whether it was gauzy, nostalgic tales of an America that used to be or heroic stories of brave young pilots going down with their planes or a heart-wrenching account of how he filmed the liberation of the Nazi death camps, the Gipper could spin a yarn like no one else.

His critics (and in terms of his ideology, we count ourselves among them) were forever pointing out that many of his stories were simply false. That didn't stop Reagan, and while we don't advocate making stuff up, accuracy is not the focus of this chapter. Storytelling is.

One of the ways Reagan skillfully fanned America's resentment against welfare was by telling the story of the welfare queen who'd purchased a Cadillac with government largesse. Again, the facts were all wrong, but the point was clear: hardworking Americans were the heroes, the welfare queen was the villain and the poor, beleaguered middle-class taxpayers were the victims. Reagan could have simply read a laundry list of statistics about the expansion of welfare, but he knew a story would have an immeasurably greater impact.

2. BE BRIEF

In the modern media age, brevity is more important than ever.

According to a landmark study by the sociologist Kiku Adato, in the 1968 presidential election the average sound bite—the time each candidate spoke without interruption on the network news—was 42.3 seconds. About once a week each of the three major candidates, Nixon, Humphrey and Wallace, got a full minute of talking on the news. But by the 2000 campaign the average sound bite had shrunk to just 7.8 seconds.

In 1992, Clinton was especially worried about this development. He used to rail privately that unlike Bush, who didn't want to do anything, and Perot, who only shouted bumper-sticker sound bites, he actually had sophisticated solutions to complicated problems. We would listen politely and then remind him that we were game players, not rule makers. Complaining about the shrinking sound bite is like griping about the weather; it may make you feel better for a while, but it's not going to change anything.

God's Own Sound Bite

Before his first major debate, we tried to persuade Clinton to learn to love the sound bite. Playing to Clinton's Southern Baptist roots, Paul pulled out a copy of the New Testament, which he'd been given years ago by a street preacher on campus at the University of Texas. He opened it to John 3:16, set his stopwatch and told Clinton to read it aloud:

> *For God so loved the world*
> *He gave His only begotten*
> *son so that whoever believes*
> *in Him shall not die but*
> *have everlasting life.*

There. In twenty-five words lasting 6.8 seconds Saint John had listed all the essentials of Christian theology:

- "For God . . ." Monotheism. Not "*the* Gods." Just God. It took humanity hundreds of thousands of years to come to the conclusion that there's only one Supreme Being. John 3:16 covers all that ground in two words and a fraction of one second.
- " . . . so loved the world . . ." God is not only singular and supreme but also benevolent. God is capable of affection, and on a global scale.
- " . . . He . . ." Okay, so God's a guy. If that offends you, take it up with the Author. We don't write this stuff, gals. We just report it.
- " . . . gave His only begotten son . . ." Whew. He has a son. And a begotten one at that. And God is willing to ship him to earth as a gift. That's an enormously complicated concept, fraught with ramifications. But delivered in five words.
- " . . . so that whoever believes in Him . . ." Having faith in this son is a prerequisite to what comes next.
- " . . . shall not die but have everlasting life." That's the payoff. Faith triumphs over everything—even death. No wonder believers call this the Good News.

So there it is. One sentence tells us that there is an all-powerful, all-loving deity who sent His Son to earth as an offering, that whoever accepts that offering and receives and returns that love will not perish when he or she dies but will instead live forever. Now you can understand why the guys in the rainbow Afros hold up the signs that say JOHN 3:16 in the end zone during football games.

Back to our story. Feeling extraordinarily smug, Paul

then delivered the punch line to Clinton: "Governor, if the Lord God can explain all the important tenets of Christianity in 6.7 seconds, surely you can tell us if you're for the balanced-budget amendment."

That exercise had no discernible effect on Bill Clinton.

Just kidding. While he never fully lost his penchant for loquacity, Clinton ultimately made peace with the sound bite, which helped him communicate his message through the media to the American people.

(By the way, none of this is meant to demean or diminish the power and beauty and to our minds the truth of John 3:16. Both of your authors are practicing Catholics who believe that message to be true. But no matter what religion you are, you should be able to recognize the economy and poetry of that one amazing sentence.)

How does this apply in your life? You're probably not going to be spending a lot of time wondering how to get network blowhards to shut up long enough to give you more than nine seconds on the evening news. But guess what? The people you're trying to reach have been raised in the sound-bite culture. They're used to professional politicians, admakers and entertainers getting to the point in a matter of seconds. You need to do the same. You can't expect people who only listen to their president for a few seconds to listen to you for an hour and a half.

Smart people think that sophistication and brevity are mutually exclusive. That's one of the many reasons we hate smart people.

Smart people like to say things that sound smart but are in reality profoundly stupid. Like "I could never live my life by a sound bite." (These are usually people who aren't doing much of a job living their life by anything, by the way.) They prefer scholarly tracts or twelve-step programs or psychotherapy. Fine. Whatever floats your boat. And, truth be told, there's probably a lot of wisdom in all of that.

But what if you took a different tack? What if you said "I'm going to throw all that crap out and live my life and raise my kids according to a sound bite"? Pretty radical, right? Maybe even stupid, don't you think?

"Do unto others as you would have them do unto you."

But that's different, you say. That's not merely a sound bite, that's the Golden Rule.

One person's sound bite is another person's Golden Rule. You could lead a good life and raise good children if you relied only on that sound bite and nothing more. There's more wisdom and more truth and more of a challenge in that one little sound bite than in all of the self-help manuals or philosophy texts you could read in a lifetime.

Crafting Your Own Sound Bite

Of course, sound bites like John 3:16 and the Golden Rule don't come along every day. Many of us believe they were divinely inspired. We're not saying that when you're pitching a new product or making a cold call or running a state senate race you've got to be as perfectly pithy as God Almighty. We'll cut you some slack. And since you've shelled out the $23.00 to buy this book, we'll let you in on some of the tricks of the trade we've picked up during our own lifelong Sound Bite Safari:

- **We hear with our ears but we listen with our minds.**
  For reasons that more sophisticated medical and psychological experts could tell you, the human mind more readily retains information if it's presented in certain ways.

  Contrasting pairs are memorable: "Ask not what your country can do for you; ask what you can do for your country." That works far better than, say: "Your obligations as a citizen are vital. Far more vital, indeed, than the obligations the nation as a whole owes to you as an individual."

- **Three may not be company, but it is a sound bite.**
  For many of the same reasons that the mind retains information presented in contrasting pairs, we also tend to remember information presented in groups of three. Don't ask us why, but one's an anecdote, two's a pair (see above), and four's a list. If you've got ten, they'd better be commandments or we ain't going to remember them. (Course, not a whole lot of folks can actually name all

Ten Commandments, either.) So make your list a group of three: "Veni, vidi, vici." Did Julius Caesar *really* need to tell us he came, he saw and he conquered? Doesn't coming somewhere suggest seeing it as well? And you can't very well conquer a place you haven't been to and haven't seen, can you? So wouldn't it have been more economical to say, "France. Conquered it"? Perhaps. But we wouldn't be repeating it a couple thousand years later if he had.

- **Surprise 'em.** Memorable things (especially funny things) have some element of surprise; they're not what we expect. For a variety of other reasons, it's even better for that twist to be self-deprecating. When James wrote "It's the Economy, Stupid" on that sign in the War Room, he wasn't calling voters stupid. It was a reference to all of his fellow "geniuses" on the campaign staff not to take themselves too seriously, not to get too cute and not to allow their supposed sophistication to get in the way of a simple strategic objective.

- **Keep it simple, smarty.** That sign in the War Room only had three things: CHANGE VERSUS MORE OF THE SAME, IT'S THE ECONOMY, STUPID and DON'T FORGET HEALTH CARE. (See, another group of three.) We could have run on a hundred things; Lord knows Clinton had more solutions than the nation had problems. A good rule of thumb, whether you're writing your corporate mission statement or your campaign's announcement speech, is that for every thing you add, you should subtract something else. Remember the great scene in *Amadeus* in which the emperor says he can't listen to Mozart's music because it contains "too many notes"? The emperor theo-

JAMES CARVILLE & PAUL BEGALA

rizes that the human ear can only hear so many notes at a time and thus Mozart's music failed because it overwhelmed him. That may be nonsense in the music world, but it makes great sense in the message world. Be ruthless when you edit. Trim and trim and trim some more. Keep it short and keep it simple.

- **Self-deprecation works.** When James was swinging into action to help Hillary Clinton in her 2000 Senate campaign, he didn't announce that the world's greatest political consultant was coming out of retirement to help a friend. So James created a new, self-deprecating moniker, Corporal Cueball—reflecting both his tonsorially challenged pate and his rank in the Marine Corps. (Hey, don't laugh. Being a corporal made James the highest-ranking military official in the Clinton administration.) People loved the name, and before he knew it, *Time* magazine had created a hilarious cartoon image of a bald-headed, crazed Marine à la Rambo with the title Corporal Cueball. The drawing now hangs on the wall of James's office, an enduring monument to the power of a self-deprecating sound bite. (In truth, Hillary and her team won that campaign on their own and didn't need or receive all that much help from James. His use of self-deprecation probably helped dampen any possible resentment from the New York campaign staff that was doing all the work, while also allowing James to help in his own way without attracting undue attention.)

The Sound Bite Hall of Fame

Here's a brief collection of some of our favorites, each of which makes a powerful point in well under nine seconds.

"As I would not be a slave, I would not be a slave owner." Abraham Lincoln

"Give me liberty or give me death." Patrick Henry

"We hold these truths to be self-evident: that all men are created equal; that they are endowed by their Creator with certain inalienable rights; that among these rights are life, liberty and the pursuit of happiness." Thomas Jefferson, in the Declaration of Independence

"Let's do it." Gary Gilmore, facing a Utah firing squad, when he was asked if he had any last words

"Honey, I forgot to duck." Ronald Reagan to his wife, Nancy, after being shot by John Hinckley

"The graveyards are filled with indispensable men." Charles de Gaulle

"Leave the gun. Take the cannoli." Clemenza from *The Godfather*

"Change is certain; progress is not." British historian E. H. Carr

"This nation, before this decade is out, will send a man to the moon and return him safely to earth." John F. Kennedy

"We're on a mission from God." Jake and Elwood Blues

"I feel your pain." Bill Clinton, to a man with AIDS who heckled and interrupted Clinton's speech in New York

"That woman who knew that I had dyslexia—I never interviewed her." George W. Bush

"We have nothing to fear but fear itself." Franklin Delano Roosevelt

"Golf is a game of luck. The more I practice, the luckier I get." Ben Hogan

"It's not gonna be an orgy. It's a toga party." Boone from *Animal House*

3. BE EMOTIONAL

Although he had his ups and downs, Bill Clinton had the highest sustained popularity of any president since political polling started back in 1948. There were many reasons for his popularity, the strong economy over which he presided being first among them. But even more enduring than any of his policy initiatives, Clinton's popularity was driven and undergirded by his ability to connect emotionally with the American people.

Although he's a terribly bright man, Clinton's greatest gift is not his intellect. It's his empathy. And while the smarty-pants set in Washington used to snicker at it, the American people got it when he said "I feel your pain."

Chances are, you're no Bill Clinton. That's okay. You can still find ways to put emotion into your argument.

Before he became a United States senator, Frank Lautenberg was a corporate CEO. His firm, ADP, was a pioneer of the computer age. And like most businesspeople, especially those in technical fields, Frank thrived on facts. And as a politician, well, let's just say he was no Clinton.

As a senator, he became a champion of the environment, mastering the arcane and impenetrable technicalities of environmental legislation. But when it came time to run for reelection, Lautenberg had a hard time translating his many environmental accomplishments into language his constituents could understand. He'd stand in a town hall meeting in Verona, New Jersey, and talk about how he'd secured $4.5 billion in new authorizations for RCRA—and wonder why his audience would fall asleep.

So we went to work to emotionalize Lautenberg's message. It wasn't hard. Turns out there was a little girl named Amy Knox who lived in Mt. Holly, New Jersey. Amy was battling cancer, a disease she believed she'd contracted because she lived near a toxic site. Little Amy was a tough, brave kid. She'd started a community group called PUKE, People United for a Klean Environment, and had written to her senator asking for support. Lautenberg had offered her help and encouragement, doing everything a good senator should do—except take credit for his work.

From the moment we found out about Amy, we banished all jargon from Lautenberg's stump speech and replaced it with the story of a little girl's courage. "When I'm on the floor of the Senate," Lautenberg would say, "and the big polluters and their pin-striped lobbyists are trying to use our state as their dumping ground, I think of Amy Knox."

Lautenberg never did become a gifted communicator. He was professionally awkward and personally difficult. But he was able to use emotion to forcefully communicate his message—and to win reelection. If he could do it, you can, too.

4. BE UNIQUE

The mutually exclusive nature of political campaigns requires politicians to offer a message that is unique. They can't say the same thing as their opponent, since the point of the exercise is to draw distinctions that force a choice.

Most commercial decisions are not as completely exclusive as voting. Still, it's useless to communicate the selfsame message as your competitor, but you'd be surprised how many people do. Every time we hear a politician say, "Vote for me because I love my wife and my children and I want to serve our great state," our B.S. indicator goes off. Why? Not only because a politician who pontificates about his family like that is setting himself up for a fall, but also because loving your wife and your state is hardly unique.

Here's our test: Pull your message out of the printer. Now read it and pretend that you're the competition. If you can deliver that message with equal credibility, it ain't a message. If both Diet Coke and Diet Pepsi have one calorie, it doesn't make a lot of sense to harp on the caloric content. So Coke devised an ad campaign around the slogan, "Just for the Taste of It," which told its audience that the key distinction was that Diet Coke tastes better than Diet Pepsi.

The key is to focus on a unique feature of your message that is also a deal-closer. One of our favorite examples is the old Hebrew National ad. Hebrew National wanted to distinguish itself from its competition by highlighting its kosher status—and in so doing convince a nonkosher audience that a kosher hot dog would be more healthful. So, although hot dogs are not exactly known for their health benefits, Hebrew National made ads featuring Uncle Sam holding a hot dog and looking to heaven while the announcer explained that Hebrew National exceeded all government health regulations, concluding with the famous tag line: "We have to answer to a higher authority."

That was a message that the not-exactly-kosher folks at Oscar Mayer couldn't use.

5. BE RELEVANT

Politicians often get so wrapped up in their own Washington jargon, or their own personal or political agendas, that they fail to ask one of the most basic questions of any message: So what? The "So what" test should tell you whether what you're talking about, or how you're saying it, is of any relevance to your audience.

The first politician who succeeded in making the budget deficit relevant was Ross Perot. Before him, most politicians who were concerned about it discussed the deficit in technical fiscal terms. That kind of impenetrable jargon is what allowed Ronald Reagan to dismiss worries about the deficit by saying, "I am not worried about our deficit. It's big enough to take care of itself."[1]

In the 1992 campaign, however, Perot did not discuss the deficit simply in technical terms. He saw it as a systemic failure of modern politics. He spoke of "cleaning out the barn," and the deficit was example number one of the kind of mess that was piling up in that barn. Perot also applied his gift for making technical issues relevant to normal Americans to the subject of trade; he spoke about job losses and unfair foreign competition and that memorable "giant sucking sound" of jobs going to Mexico under the North American Free Trade Agreement. On the issue of campaign finance reform, Perot again was able to make a connection in ways that career politicians had not done before.

So why did Perot crash and burn so spectacularly in the 1992 campaign, dropping out one day, returning another day? In part because he fell into irrelevancy. As the heat of the campaign reached its predictable white-hot pitch, Perot melted a little. Perot claimed that Black Panthers hired by the Vietcong had tried to storm his home, only to be driven off by his guard dogs, one of whom had bitten an invading

Panther. "When the dog came back," Perot said, "he had a piece of a guy's fanny in his mouth." (We always feared the election would be decided by a piece of ass, but this is not what Perot had in mind.) But when the press contacted the man who had been Perot's director of security at the time, he said that, to the best of his knowledge, nothing like that had ever taken place.[2] And it wasn't as if Viet Cong–sponsored Black Panther raids were so common in Dallas that it could have gone unnoticed.

Perot also accused President George H. W. Bush of having had a secret plan to disrupt his daughter's wedding in Texas.[3]

Paul got married in a Texas wedding, so he can say this: There are only two ways you can disrupt a Texas wedding— show up sober and leave with your own date. That'd be a helluva disruption. But short of that, Texans pride themselves on rip-roaring celebrations.

Set aside the problem that those kinds of stories began to convince some voters that ol' H. Ross might be about a half-a-bubble off plumb. They were also irrelevant. Does a plan to invade Perot's home or disrupt his daughter's wedding have any effect on you, your family, your life or your country? Of course not. And certainly nothing like the effect of the deficit or trade or campaign reform.

Bush senior also fell victim to irrelevancy, though not on as grand or nutty a scale. By the end of the campaign, Bush and his team had a new slogan: Annoy the Media, Reelect Bush. They actually had hats and signs and T-shirts with that slogan emblazoned on it. Can you imagine that a single voter looked at Clinton, who was focusing like a laser beam on the economy, and Bush, who was whining about the media, and said, "You know, Harvey, I do think we need some new ideas on the economy. But I'm gonna vote for Bush just to piss off Sam Donaldson."

Make your message relevant to the needs, concerns and dreams of your audience or your audience will tune you out.

6. REPEAT YOUR MESSAGE RELENTLESSLY

If the mantra of success in real estate is "location, location, location," the mantra of communicating is "repetition, repetition, repetition." Do you know why politicians repeat the same basic message thousands of times? Because it works. Because we're not hanging on their every word—and for that brief moment when we do pay attention to them, they want to say exactly what will get them elected. They're not sure when that moment will come, so they repeat their message over and over. (Or at least the good ones do.)

George W. Bush was a relentlessly disciplined candidate, returning again and again to his basic issues. In his first major campaign, against Ann Richards for governor in 1994, Bush ran on four issues and four issues only. Seven years later we can still repeat them from memory—that's how often Bush repeated them on the campaign trail. They were education reform, welfare reform, juvenile justice reform and tort reform. He repeated those four issues so often it drove the press corps crazy. Finally one exasperated reporter asked Bush what his fifth goal as governor would be. "Pass the first four," he said.

When he defeated Richards and became governor, Bush's message discipline paid off. He was legitimately able to claim a mandate for his agenda. As a presidential candidate, Bush ran a similarly disciplined campaign. While Al Gore often seemed to flop about like a fish on a deck in search of a core rationale for his candidacy, Bush did a pretty good job of sticking to his "compassionate conservative" and "uniter not a divider" themes.

To be sure, we're not Junior's biggest fans. But if he could succeed by endless, disciplined repetition, imagine what you can do. (If this were a partisan book, here is where we would quote from that old auto safety ad: "You can learn a lot from a dummy." Thank goodness this isn't a partisan book.)

Repetition Under Fire

It's easy for a politician to stay "on message" when all he's doing is reading from a TelePrompTer. And it should be easy for you to stick to your basic message in a prepared text or report or memo. The true test of message discipline, however, is the ability to repeat the message when someone's trying to draw you off-message. That's when a fanatical commitment to returning again and again to your basic point is essential.

Think of it as a game. You've been dropped into the middle of a rhetorical maze. Your job is to get back to "home base"—your message—in as few words as possible. The greatest example we ever saw did not come from a politician or a business tycoon or a skilled academic. It came from a fighter.

On November 9, 1996, Evander Holyfield stunned the boxing world and won the heavyweight championship with an eleventh-round technical knockout (TKO) against the heavily favored and seemingly indestructible Mike Tyson. Still dripping with sweat and panting from his exertion, Holyfield was interviewed in the ring by "the Fight Doctor," Ferdie Pacheco, who was providing commentary on Pay-Per-View. Normally such interviews are brief and uneventful. The fighter is usually too tired or too inarticulate (or both) to shed any meaningful light on the bout he's just completed. But this interview was different. In addition to being a fighter, Evander Holyfield was a man on a mission, and his mission was to deliver a message to the millions of people who all of a sudden wanted to hear from him.

Here's how the interview went.

PACHECO: That's one of the biggest surprises in boxing I've ever had.

HOLYFIELD: Well, you know, I give glory to God, and I want for everybody to know that you can't choose against God. You can choose against me anytime, but when God is involved, Jesus is alive and He's the credit for it, and I thank God.

PACHECO: Why did you guarantee it with such assurance?

HOLYFIELD: Because anytime when someone puts God up there, my God is the only true God and everything must bow to God.

PACHECO: Well, you know, apart from that, apart from religion because God is here, I hope for all of us. I hope He's a just God. But let's get off that, let's get on to boxing: How did you fight such a brilliant fight?

HOLYFIELD: Well, you know, I live by the Spirit of God, and like I told everybody, whatever the Spirit leads me to do that's what I would do. And it wasn't nothing so much that I did. Everybody knew that I was a wash-up, but with God I'm not washed up.

PACHECO: Did you see him getting tired? Did you think you could take him on at the end?

HOLYFIELD: It wasn't about tired. It was about what the Lord wanted me to do. And each and every round—I went out there and I fought competitive each round. I wasn't giving up anything. I went to the point to take one round at a time. I realized how competitive he was, and he caught me with good shots, but I thank God for allowing me to absorb the shots.

Fifteen times—in response to just four questions—Holyfield returned to his basic message. He wanted to tell the world about his relationship with God, so he told them. Again and again Holyfield had the presence of mind to slip the reporter's narrow, tactical questions and deliver the message he wanted to deliver.

Holyfield doesn't have an Ivy League education. He wasn't reading off of focus-group-tested talking points. He did not have the benefit of a TelePrompTer. He simply stood, alone, wearing nothing but a pair of shorts and a pair of boxing gloves, and gave a performance of message discipline as impressive in its way as his destruction of Tyson in the ring had been.

This exchange is also instructive in that it is a classic example of how an interview develops. Notice how Pacheco begins with an open-ended comment, inviting Holyfield to say whatever he wants. Pachero may as well have begun by saying, "Anything on your mind, champ?" But with each question Pacheco gets more specific. And then he gets annoyed. This seems foolish to us; given that Holyfield had just finished kicking Mike Tyson's ass, we have a hard time imagining the new champ was very intimidated by "the Fight Doctor." But that's the nature of interviewing. Pacheco wants Holyfield to be an analyst. Holyfield wants to be an evangelist. It's a contest of wills, and Holyfield wins in a knockout.

Communications skills aren't exactly central to being the heavyweight champion of the world. But even in that business they help. People are busy. They have short attention spans. Telling a story, being brief, using emotion, saying something no one else can, keeping your message relevant to your audience and repeating it until it penetrates will make you a better communicator. These devices have helped two ugly southern goofballs get on national television with surprising regularity. Imagine what they can do for you.

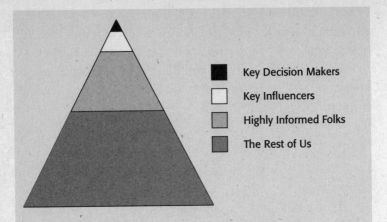

Key Decision Makers

Key Influencers

Highly Informed Folks

The Rest of Us

The Pyramid of Public Awareness

It turns out that with most issues, whether it's politics or NBA basketball or women's shoes, public awareness can be plotted on a pyramid.

At the top there is the 1 percent. They are the key decision makers. In politics they're the members of Congress, the president, the Cabinet, etc. In the NBA it's the commissioner, the owners, the players and the refs. In women's shoes it's . . . oh, hell . . . what do we know? (We'll get to why that's instructive in a minute.)

Beneath the top 1 percent is about 5 percent of key influencers. Again, to use politics as the example, they're the staffers and the lobbyists and the big-shot pundits who have direct access to and influence on the key decision makers. In the NBA we suppose it's the sportswriters, the network executives, the agents, etc. In women's shoes . . . clueless again.

The next level on the pyramid is about 15 percent. They're the highly informed folks. In politics they're the folks who read the political and governmental news coverage in the paper each day. They tune in to CNN and news programs. They write their congressional member and they darn sure vote. In the NBA it's the hardcore fans: the season-ticket holders, the folks who follow the team on TV each night and in the paper each morning. The kinds of people who call players by their first name or their nickname: "Did you see what Zo did to Penny last night?" In women's shoes it's . . . the women who buy a lot of shoes. But we're just guessing here.

And below that, filling in the bulk of the pyramid, is the other 79 percent of us. Mass opinion. And pretty darn clueless. If you're an exclusive, elite enterprise, you can probably afford to write those folks off. For reasons of lack of income or interest or whatever, you don't need them. That's fine.

But if you do, if, like a politician, your fate, your future and your fortune are in the hands of those 79 percent, you'd better be able to reach them. But they haven't clued in. Why?

The *Washington Post* did a national poll a few years back. The poll found that fewer than three in ten Americans could name their member of Congress. Only 9 percent of Americans could identify William Rehnquist as the man who presides over the Supreme Court, but 54 percent of Americans knew that Judge Wapner presided over the People's Court.

Does this mean we're America the Ignorant? A lot of folks in Washington smugly concluded it did. But there's another theory that explains it better. It's called Rational Ignorance, and it says that people today are bombarded by information: news, advertising, entertainment, gossip, all coming at us faster and heavier than ever before in human history. We daresay a person in the twenty-first century probably receives more information in an average week than an ordinary twelfth-century person did in his or her whole lifetime.

One logical response to that sensory overload is to erect barriers. We set up filters that keep information we don't want or don't need or can't use from filling up our increasingly scarce time and attention. So we rationally (if sometimes unconsciously) choose to be ignorant about lots of things that others think are vitally important. We know lots of women who can't believe that we're as totally and completely ignorant as we are about women's footwear.

It's important to keep in mind that ignorance and stupidity are not the same thing. We don't think we're stupid because we don't know anything about women's shoes; just ignorant. And a guy who doesn't spend much time worrying about how Judge Wapner's doing on the Supreme Court isn't stupid, either. He's rationally decided that he'll expend his mental energy on how he's going to pay for those braces on his thirteen-year-old daughter, how he's going to meet next month's tuition bill, car payment, mortgage and all the other bills.

The challenge for you, the communicator, is to be able to reach into that big pot of rationally ignorant people and convince them to alter their filter enough to engage with your issue or topic. Keeping in mind that the people who are ignorant about your passion aren't stupid—in fact, in many ways they're smarter than you—is a good start.

Rule 8

Work Your Ass Off

The Big Secret

Like so many books filled with advice on how to succeed, this one has a secret. Now that you've paid for the book and plowed through nearly all of it, it's time you learned our secret. The key to success. The Rosetta Stone that will unlock the mysteries of achievement. Are you ready? Drumroll, please.

Work your ass off.

We're serious. Both of us can recall during law school wishing that the professors would just tell us the rules we had to memorize. But rules change, and good law professors understand that if they teach you how to think like a lawyer—and work like a lawyer—you'll be able to memorize all the rules you need later on.

There are no shortcuts. If you're looking for the equivalent of winning the lottery, you've come to the wrong place. Napoleon once said that God is on the side of the big battalions. He was right. In the nonmilitary context, God is on the side of the hard workers.

The people who succeed tend to get up earlier in the morning; they tend to go to bed late at night. They tend to put in more hours, more productively, than others. Of course, there are exceptions. You may have known someone in school who could screw around all semester then ace the exam without even cracking the book. If you're one of those people, you've just wasted $23.00. You don't need this book. But if you're not one of those rare souls to whom success comes without effort, welcome to the human race.

Both of your authors are Catholic, so it pains us to say this: There's something to be said for the Protestant work ethic. Here are some of our favorite examples of people who are where they are because they just plain outwork the competition.

THE HAMMER

Of all the politicians you can imagine, we probably dislike Tom DeLay the most. As the House Republican Whip he's the leader of his party's forces in the House of Representatives. He is politically radical and personally unpleasant. He has never been accused of having charm, much less charisma. He's no dummy, but no one would ever confuse him with an intellectual. He's a flat-footed orator given to hyperbolic rants. Even he admits that his looks are so severe that he looks downright scary, even when he tries to smile. And his strategic vision has been called into question as he has marched his party colleagues, lemminglike, off a series of cliffs from Clinton's impeachment to trying to repeal environmental protections.

In sum, DeLay is as Hobbes described life: "Nasty, brutish and short."

And yet he is the most powerful man in the House of

Representatives and perhaps in all of Washington. The Speaker, Dennis Hastert, was DeLay's campaign manager in his race for Whip. He was chosen to be Speaker by DeLay, who theoretically holds a lesser title but is obviously the man in charge. How does DeLay do it?

Let us count the ways. First, and most important, he uses power with a ruthlessness that would make old Joe Stalin proud. Second, money. DeLay strongarms lobbyists, political action committees, corporations—especially really lovely folks like cigarette companies—into giving to the GOP. He has raised untold tens of millions of dollars for his right-wing causes.

We don't like how DeLay exercises power, and we don't like the system of special-interest fund-raising he has mastered. But there's a third reason DeLay is so successful; a reason less reported by the media.

He works his ass off.

Tom DeLay went from being a pest-control man in Sugar Land, Texas, to being one of the most powerful people in the most powerful nation in the history of the world in large measure because he just flat-out outworked everyone else. Other members of Congress are surely as conservative (though, truth be told, not many). And too many congressmen have proved adept at shaking the money tree. But from the moment he wakes up in the morning till the moment his head hits the pillow at night, DeLay is a man at work.

DeLay became Whip after traveling the country in a carefully planned campaign to raise funds to help his fellow Republicans. He traveled thousands of miles, attended innumerable events and raised millions. When the Republican revolution of 1994 swept the GOP into power with 73 new members, DeLay was ready. He easily defeated the handpicked candidate of Newt Gingrich—when Gingrich was at the height of his power. "DeLay did far and away the best job of securing commitments from the new members, and that was decisive—pivotal, actually—in the outcome of the whip's race," said Rep. Frank Riggs of California.[1]

Once in charge of the whip operation, DeLay turned it into a powerhouse. Theoretically charged with counting votes for the Speaker, DeLay uses his whip operation to, literally, whip members into line. He manipulates, massages and manhandles his fellow congressmen through his whip organization: 67 members—nearly a third of all the Republicans in Congress—report directly to DeLay. "He knows when to say 'We can't have that person talk to that other guy because they don't get along, or their wives hate each other,' one unnamed source told *The Hill,* a trade paper on Capitol Hill. "He knows everything about these people. And he appreciates the subtleties of not only who should talk to a person, but how to talk to them, and when to talk to them."[2]

DeLay himself described his system to *Texas Monthly* thusly: "We try to find out early if a member has a problem with a bill and we fix it in committee if we can. If that doesn't work, I try to use my personal relationship with a member." If that doesn't work, out comes The Hammer. "We have one member who loves to travel abroad," he told the magazine with what the interviewer described as a thin smile. "We told him that from now on, he can go on his own nickel."[3]

TIM RUSSERT

If you've seen the classic movie *Broadcast News,* you might think the modern electronic media is filled with characters like the one played by William Hurt: beautiful, vacuous people who don't know a news story from a fairy tale. Empty heads who spend more time on their hair than they do reading. Mannequins whose only gift is the ability to read from a TelePrompTer brief snippets other folks have written for them while gazing forcefully into the camera.

If you think that, you don't know Tim Russert.

Tim ain't the prettiest thing you've ever seen. He could stand to lose a few pounds, and we doubt he's ever been on the business end of a blow-dryer. Nor does he have the Ivy League pedigree that might make up for not being so easy on the eyes. He went to tiny John Carroll University and Cleveland-Marshall College of Law. And he hasn't climbed the greasy pole by getting a boost from his family. Far from being wealthy and connected, Tim's father, known to everyone in Buffalo, New York, as Big Russ, gave his son more grit than gold. Big Russ quit school in tenth grade to fight in World War II, and when he returned, he worked two jobs for thirty-nine years: one as a truck driver for the *Buffalo News,* the other on a garbage truck.

Today, Big Russ's son Tim is the most feared and respected television journalist in Washington. He stands astride the colossus of *Meet the Press,* bludgeoning Cabinet secretaries and eating congressmen for breakfast. Both among Beltway elites and among real people, Russert's show is number one. He is widely credited with having revolutionized Sunday-morning political talk shows. You know you've really arrived in Washington when you've been grilled by Russert.

How did he get there? Why is this unlikely, untelegenic Everyman the king of Sunday morning? Because he works so damn hard. He's always there to take a phone call from a source or hear a complaint from a spin doctor. When he's trying to get the newsmaker of the week on his show, he's like a cross between a hemorrhoid and a toothache; you just can't get rid of the guy.

Russert's formula is not complicated, but it is rigorous. "When I took over *Meet the Press* in 1991," he says, "I went to see Lawrence Spivak [the longtime, legendary host of *Meet the Press*]. And he told me the mission of *Meet the Press* was very simple: you learn as much as you can about your guest and his or her position on the issue. Then you take the other side."

Carrying out that devil's advocate mission requires an enormous amount of work. Russert begins each day at 6 A.M. and reads seven newspapers (*The New York Times, The Washington Post, The Wall Street Journal,* the New York *Daily News, The Washington Times, USA Today* and the *Los Angeles Times*). He then channel-surfs through the morning news programs on TV: *Today, Good Morning America, CBS This Morning, Imus in the Morning,* even CSPAN.

Russert also reads all three news weeklies and as many opinion journals as he can get his hands on. "You have to understand people's perspectives," he says. "What is the liberal view? What is the conservative view? What is the neoconservative view?" And so he devours *The Weekly Standard, The New Republic, Commentary, The Nation* and *The New York Review of Books,* among others.

Russert's also a fan of the tomes put out by Washington think tanks. "Washington is just so rich with the Brookings Institution and the Cato Institute and all the rest. They all have publications on a wide variety of issues. The thing about being a journalist is you have the privilege and the luxury of having access to all these people who are truly experts and specialists in a whole variety of areas," he says.

But in addition to being a policy wonk, Russert is a newshound and a political junkie. As Washington bureau chief of NBC News, he's on the phone constantly, with the brass in New York, with reporters and producers in the field and, most important of all, with sources. Russert talks to at least fifty people every day. Some offer tidbits with a partisan ax to grind, so Russert insists on original sourcing, not hearsay. Others simply want to spin. "You never know what twist is going to open the jar," he says. "So you're always talking to people, establishing relationships, knowing where people are and how they are involved with certain things."

One of Russert's biggest scoops was when he broke the story that Bob Dole was going to resign from the United States Senate in order to pursue the presidency full-time. "The other networks were saying, 'Not true. It can't be.' I had a pit in my stomach. But I had gotten it hard. A guy called me and told me and then I called two other people whom I know and I trust and they said, 'Absolutely. It's coming down, it's happening.' And it did happen."

Russert's hard work had yielded him three solid sources on the biggest story in Washington before his competitors had found even one. Dole later marveled to Russert, "Where did you get it? The only person I told was Elizabeth." Russert replied, "I'm not going to tell you if I talked to your wife."

That daily routine is just the buildup for the Big Kahuna of Russert's life: Sunday's show. Once Russert settles on a guest, he reads everything he can about him or her. Everything. Profiles in the politician's local paper, interviews with his mother and especially transcripts of prior interviews. "I prepare for a three-hour program," Russert says despite the fact that *Meet* only runs about forty-four minutes, excluding commercials. "I try to verse myself in every particular issue. And sometimes I only get to one issue or two issues and all the rest are just left on the sidelines because the discussion is good or we're making news or I think the country is seeing that the person is inconsistent and really doesn't believe in what they're saying.

"The secret really is preparation and persistence," Russert says. "You prepare, prepare, prepare, and then when you go in there, don't be afraid to ask the followup questions, sometimes two, three, four times."

When the guest is a really major newsmaker, Russert takes his game up still another notch. Before he interviewed GOP presidential nominee George W. Bush and Democratic presidential nominee Al Gore for an hour each during the 2000 campaign, Russert prepared an eight-page, single-spaced outline on each man. He thought of every topic that might come up, every position they'd ever taken, every issue they'd ever ducked, everything they'd been asked and everything they'd never been asked. He logged sixty hours of prep time for each interview.

His thoroughness paid off. In his interview Gore candidly admitted he'd changed his position on gun control—something he'd been unwilling to do in the past—but stumbled badly when Russert asked him about his fundraising controversies at the Buddhist temple and if he'd execute a pregnant woman.

In his interview, Bush for the first time named ultra-conservative Supreme Court Justices Antonin Scalia and Clarence Thomas as his ideal appointees for the high court, a revelation that must have startled and worried the moderate "soccer mom" women Bush was trying to woo with his "compassionate conservative" rhetoric.

For his thoroughness and fairness in those interviews, Russert was awarded the prestigious Joan Shorenstein Barone Award from the Radio and Television Correspondents Association.

The depth of his preparation requires a commitment that the devoutly Catholic Russert likens to a "vocation." He does not go out on Saturday night. "I'm afraid to go out," he says with a laugh. "I'm afraid to have a beer. I don't want anything to detract from absolute focus and total attention." Instead he spends most of the day with his son, Luke, goes to Mass, then locks himself away for the rest of the evening, sitting in his favorite rocking chair and going through the next day's interviews in his mind.

At the end of the day, Russert attributes his success to the blue-collar work ethic and sensibilities he was raised with back in Buffalo. As a young staff aide to Senator Daniel Patrick Moynihan, Russert was awed—and a little intimidated—by the highfalutin intellectual debates of Moynihan's Ivy League aides. Russert felt so out of place, so inadequate, he offered to quit. "Moynihan put his arm around me and said, 'Let me tell you something: whatever they know you can learn. What you know they will never know. That's why you're from Buffalo.' That changed my life. I realized that all my summer jobs—my dad got me a job as a garbageman during the summer, I made pizzas, I drove taxis—made me who I am."

HILLARY

Senator Hillary Rodham Clinton is one of the few people on earth who is known all around the world by her first name only—like Cher and Madonna. Hillary endured so much for so long—the vicious attacks from her critics on the right, the strain of life in the White House, the constant pressure to use her daughter to "soften" her image and of course her husband's misbehavior—that no one would have blamed her if she had used her fame and influence after being First Lady to make a fortune and do charitable work in her spare time.

But Hillary decided to run for the Senate . . . in a state she'd never lived in.

As if you didn't know, we love Hillary about as much as we dislike Tom DeLay. But they have this in common: They both work their tails off. Although she's enormously talented, she lacks Bill Clinton's natural, raw political skills. (Even the comparison is unfair. Bill Clinton is the Michael Jordan, Tiger Woods and Hank Aaron of politics all rolled into one.) Hillary's unwillingness to gush about her private life and her steadfast commitment to preserving her marriage have made her a target to some on both the left and the right. And she ran for the Senate first against the popular mayor of New York City, Rudy Giuliani, then against Rick Lazio, an attractive, moderate Republican congressman who'd spent his whole life as a New Yorker.

And yet she won.

She won for a very simple reason: She worked harder. Conventional wisdom called for her to spend her time in heavily Democratic New York City and the traditionally swing areas of the suburbs and to ignore the reliably Republican region upstate. But Hillary's work ethic would not allow her to write off an entire region. She visited every single one of the state's sixty-two counties (the first politician in memory to do so), campaigned nonstop for sixteen months, had three debates, went through two opponents, and (as she joked on election night) wore out six black pantsuits.

New York is a Democratic state, to be sure. Even with that built-in advantage, Hillary won by one of the biggest margins in the state's history, an astonishing, smashing 18-point victory. There's no doubt that her intelligence and her stands on the issues helped. When you read the newspapers across the state that endorsed her, however, another theme emerges: Hillary's phenomenal work ethic. Far from parachuting in as if she were royalty returning from exile, Hillary worked her tail off. Look at what the papers said:

- "Through the collection of firsthand stories, she learned about economic deprivation, energy costs, taxes, health crises and troubled schools. She came out of those grueling months knowing more about the state than most candidates who qualify by birth as what Mr. Lazio calls 'real New Yorkers'." *The New York Times*[4]
- "She has run on the issues, and much harder, with more verve, imagination, intelligence and spirit. But the greatest, and most decisive, difference is that she has pledged to work for Rochester." *Rochester Democrat and Chronicle*[5]
- "But [Lazio's] grasp and vision of New York doesn't match Mrs. Clinton's. She started traveling the state almost a year before he did. Her legwork and homework have paid off. . . . Her knowledge of this large and extremely diverse state and her advocacy for government policies on its behalf are most impressive. Both are the result of a tireless campaign." *Albany Times-Union*[6]

Since arriving in the Senate, Hillary has only redoubled her efforts. Here's her schedule from a typical day (with thanks to Jim Kennedy of Hillary's staff for sharing it with us):

8:45 A.M. Leave Washington for flight to Wheeler-Sack Airfield at Fort Drum in New York
10:30 A.M. Arrive at Wheeler-Sack Airfield, where she'll

be greeted by the commanding general and his wife

10:40 A.M.   Tour the McEwen Education Center and library at Fort Drum

11:00 A.M.   Tour the Army Support Complex at Fort Drum and meet with families of Fort Drum base personnel

11:45 A.M.   Lunch with the command staff of the base and community leaders

12:35 P.M.   Meet with the Fort Drum Regional Liaison Organization (the group that links the community with the base; they'll discuss the issue of potential base closing legislation, how important Fort Drum is to the north country economy, how the soldiers and their families participate in the life of the community, etc.)

1:30 P.M.   Meet with soldiers preparing to deploy to Kosovo and Bosnia. Also will observe readiness training exercises

2:20 P.M.   Press availability

2:45 P.M.   Helicopter tour of Fort Drum, and brief visit with the commanding general

3:35 P.M.   Meeting with the publisher of the *Watertown Times*

4:20 P.M.   Depart Fort Drum to travel to Hanno's farm in Lowville, NY

5:00 P.M.   Arrive Hanno's farm, meet with 100 people, including representatives of the Lewis County Chamber of Commerce, the local cooperative extension service, and a number of local dairy farmers to discuss agricultural issues

6:00 P.M.   Depart Hanno's farm en route to Watertown airport

6:40 P.M.	Meet with approximately 20 people to discuss the status of Essential Air Service, which serves the region
7:30 P.M.	Greet constituents in airport lobby
7:45 P.M.	Press availability at the airport
8:00 P.M.	Depart the airport for the airfield at Fort Drum
8:10 P.M.	Say good-bye to commanding general and his wife, sign pictures for local dignitaries
9:45 P.M.	Arrive D.C. Begin reading briefing books for the next day's activities, which range from legislative business in Washington to constituent service in New York

This is a far cry from the glamour and glitz of being the First Lady. And yet Hillary clearly loves it. Perhaps her work ethic comes from her days growing up in a very traditional family in suburban Chicago, where she was a Goldwater girl before her religious faith, concern for civil rights and commitment to family issues led her to the Democratic Party. "My parents instilled in me a strong appreciation for the value of hard work," she says in what may be the understatement of the century. "Throughout my life, I have worked hard—in school, in the practice of law and in my work on behalf of children and families."

Even her harshest critics concede Hillary's work ethic. Barbara Olson, who wrote a scathingly critical book about Hillary, was debating Paul on Hillary's future on CNN's *Wolf Blitzer Reports*. When Paul asserted that Hillary was a hard worker, Barbara replied: "I agree with Paul. She works harder than anyone else. And don't forget, someone's got to be the vice president candidate. And Hillary would make a great vice president candidate also." (Tragically, Barbara was killed just days later when terrorists hijacked the plane she was on and crashed it into the Pentagon, but not before Barbara heroically called her husband to warn people on the ground.)

THE IRON MAN

No discussion of the value of hard work would be complete without a tribute to Cal Ripken Jr. Now that he's retired from baseball, every sports fan knows of Ripken's remarkable longevity; how he played 2,632 consecutive games, smashing Lou Gehrig's supposedly unbreakable record; how he set records for most appearances in the All-Star game (19), most consecutive innings played without a rest (8,243) and most home runs by a shortstop (345), as well as 11 fielding records.

We know Cal by those numbers, but not enough people know how he put them up. Yes, he had terrific physical tools. He was unusually big for a shortstop (6'4"), with great range and a strong arm. But the most impressive thing about Ripken is that even after he was a bona fide superstar, he never lost his work ethic. "Practice makes perfect" was not enough for Cal. He had to modify the old saying to reflect the Ripken way: "*Perfect* practice makes perfect."

It was not enough to put in the hours, although God knows he did. Ripken insisted on making each practice as nearly perfect as possible, as demanding as it could be and more challenging and tedious than most people could stand. While most baseball players follow the time-honored rhythms of the baseball season—getting fat in the winter, shaping up during spring training and staying fit all summer to peak in the fall—Ripken stayed in shape year-round. His fitness regimen included all-out full-court basketball, with tiered games against top-notch college basketball players and former college and professional players, and with his Oriole teammates.

He hit thousands upon thousands of balls off a tee—just like a five-year-old. But unlike any five-year-old, his practice had a very serious purpose. He was the man of a thousand swings, constantly adjusting and readjusting his stance, his hands, his feet, his hips, his shoulders, his head, his chin. Hitting a few hundred balls with each new iteration until it was an unconscious groove.

Ripken didn't miss a day of work for seventeen years, and for that feat alone he has earned his spot in baseball lore. His work ethic extended to the postgame hours as well, when many an exuberant ballplayer has been known to come down from the high of a game with a little help from Jack Daniel's and whatever ladies were about. But not Rip. Sure, he'd turn in about 3 A.M. after a game, but that's because Ripken would work out for hours afterward: lifting weights, cycling, anything to give him the slightest additional edge.

And yet for all his preparation, for all his training, Ripken was not invulnerable. Just two months shy of Lou Gehrig's record for most consecutive games played, Ripken was caught in the middle of a bench-clearing brawl. Trying to keep the opposing Mariners from hurting Orioles ace Mike Mussina, Ripken twisted his knee as 1,000 pounds of baseball players collapsed on top of him in the melee. His knee, badly twisted, could not support his weight the next morning. Ripken's wife suggested that perhaps he should play just one inning—enough to record an appearance for that game—a tactic that even the fabled Gehrig had gladly employed.

But not Ripken. He played the whole game.

Ripken titled his autobiography *The Only Way I Know,*

reflecting his core values. Or as he has said, "You come to the ballpark—show up and say you want to play. And if the manager says, 'You're one of my nine guys,' then you just go out and play."

You show up. You do your job. You strive for a level of perfection. Then you get up in the morning and do it all over again. That's why, all across America, children like little Matty Carville, when asked who their favorite ballplayer is, say, "Number eight, Cal Ripken Jr."

The reason the Carville girls know Cal's name—and the reason the Begala boys wear uniforms with his number on it—is the same reason Hillary is in the Senate and Tom DeLay runs the House and Tim Russert dominates Sunday morning: They work their asses off.

Hard work can make up for a lot—lack of innate genius, grating interpersonal skills, even ugly scars and tattoos. But without a strong work ethic, even the geniuses, the charmers and the folks with flawless skin wind up losers.

Rule 9

Turn Weakness into Strength

You gotta hand it to the Greeks: They had a great sense of tragedy. In Greek tragedy the hero always had a tragic flaw that caused his downfall. And what made it so very tragic was that the flaw was inextricably intertwined with the hero's greatest gift.

And so Achilles, whose greatest gift was his near invincibility in battle, was vulnerable in one spot—his heel—which, of course, is precisely where he was struck in battle (with an arrow that conspiracy theorists believe came from the grassy knoll).

One of the reasons Greek tragedies endure is that they're true to life. So often in life people are brought low by their greatest talent. If we hear one more person lament the fact that Bill Clinton's brilliance and glibness made him feel he could talk his way out of his embarrassing affair we're going to throw up. And yet even Clinton commandos like us have to admit that there may be some truth to that notion.

But why can't it work the other way just as easily? Why can't people take their greatest weakness and use it to form their greatest strength? They can.

If James had been raised these days, he'd likely be spotted right away as what's now called an AD/HD child, for Attention Deficit/Hyperactivity Disorder. Back in Carville, Louisiana, James's mother, Miz Nippy, used to call him a toaster, because he popped up every five minutes. James wasn't exactly a standout student—unless you count his claim that he set the record for F's at LSU with 64 hours of F's. And as a lawyer he wasn't even Perry Como, much less Perry Mason.

But James learned to use his disability to his advantage. He gravitated to campaigns, where by definition no job lasts longer than one election cycle. And while he trained himself (with the help of a stint in the Marine Corps) to stay on-task, his short attention span became his greatest asset. In a world in which smart people like to bloviate, James would insist on cutting to the chase. Perhaps because of his long and undistinguished academic record, James has always prided himself on his ability to cut through technical mumbo-jumbo and present ideas and issues to voters in a way they can understand. His campaigns became known for their speed and agility—all products of a man whose mind needs quick actions and rapid stimuli. His meetings became famous for their brevity. And his mind, once derided by more conventional thinkers, is now considered to be pretty good at reacting quickly and decisively.

Paul's biggest weakness, in case you haven't guessed, is that he can be a bit of a smart-ass. While he never had to cope with the challenges of AD/HD in school, Paul was a frequent recipient of what were then called "pops"—swats on the butt administered by the not-very-enlightened faculty of John Foster Dulles Junior High School and John Foster Dulles High School (where they clearly valued consistency over creativity in naming their schools) in Sugar Land, Texas.

Once, in junior high, Paul and his friends thought it would be cool to answer the roll call by saying "whiskey" instead of "here." One day the teacher had had enough. "The next person who answers the roll 'whiskey' is going to have that word spelled out on their butts with pops," he growled. But Paul was absent that day and his classmates somehow forgot to let him in on the new rule. So the next day, when the teacher called the roll, Paul shouted, "Whiskey!" The teacher grabbed his paddle with one hand, grabbed Paul with the other and stormed out into the hall.

W POP!

H POP!

I POP!

S POP!

K POP!

Y POP!

"I hope that taught you a lesson," said the teacher. Paul's butt was on fire, but he still couldn't suppress one smart-ass comment. "Isn't 'whiskey' spelled with an *e* before the *y?*"

BAM! POP!

Fortunately (for Paul and his butt), corporal punishment is not commonly administered to political hacks. So Paul was drawn to a business where he could use his penchant for conflict and his love of ridicule to earn a living. Today those teachers back in Sugar Land who said Paul would never get anywhere with his foul mouth and his smart-aleck attitude are still shaking their heads in disbelief. They can't believe a guy can earn a living by comparing former Republican National Committee chairman Haley Barbour to Arnold Ziffel, the pig on *Green Acres,* or by saying that Bob Dole looked like the kind of guy who'd enjoy clubbing baby seals, or by calling Rush Limbaugh "lard butt."

Only in America.

Most of the great politicians were able to turn their supposed weaknesses into strengths. Jefferson was such a poor speaker, and such a brilliant writer, that he refused to stand and speak in defense of his draft of the Declaration of Independence, and his silence was more effective than any orator's eloquence. (He would later use this tactic as president, preferring to submit a written report on the State of the Union rather than giving a speech.)

Abraham Lincoln used his less-than-handsome appearance and his rough, backcountry upbringing to cultivate an image of simple decency and integrity. Lincoln's bouts with depression and the death of his son may well have given him a profound empathy for the suffering so many families endured during the Civil War.

Teddy Roosevelt had been sickly as a child, which drove him to become a more robust adult, which in turn led to his joining the army, forming the Rough Riders (gathered from the hard-drinking patrons of the Menger Hotel bar in San Antonio) and making his famous charge up San Juan Hill. Would TR have been a war hero if as a child he hadn't been a wimp? Probably not.

His cousin, Franklin Roosevelt, used his crippling polio to develop the compassion for suffering that was the hallmark of the New Deal, as well as the iron will that carried America through World War II.

Lyndon Johnson was massively insecure about being raised in rural Texas and educated at Southwest Texas State

Teachers College instead of at an Ivy League college. Perhaps that's why he had such a strong commitment to education—and especially for poor and minority kids.

Ronald Reagan was dismissed as nothing more than an actor. Edmund "Pat" Brown, the Democratic governor Reagan unseated, once reminded his audience that Reagan was an actor "and you will recall that it was an actor who assassinated Lincoln." But Reagan used his stage presence to master the theatricality of the office as had no president before him. His ability to read a script and deliver it with credibility was nothing less than superb.

And, of course, Bill Clinton. We're hopelessly biased when it comes to our friend and former boss. But if we had to analyze him we'd say his greatest weakness seemed to be the "slick" factor. He seemed to be all things to all people. (If you read biographies of FDR and Lincoln, you learn that the same thing was said about them. "Slick Abe"?) Clinton turned that into a strength by adapting to changed circumstances. With a Democratic congressional majority he passed his economic plan, crime plan, family medical leave plan and the Brady bill. With a Republican congressional majority he—slickly—adapted, passing welfare reform and putting the final touches on a balanced budget. The poor Republicans. They were so flummoxed by Clinton, they didn't know whether to wind their asses or scratch their watches.

Making Chicken Salad

A good salesperson, like a good politician, knows how to turn chicken shit into chicken salad. Anyone can sell a product if it's already exactly what the buyers think they want. Sometimes you can bluff your way through it. But it takes real talent to convince people that the thing they hated most of all is in fact the most desirable feature.

When Paul's wife, Diane, came up to Washington from Austin to pick out a house for them, the one thing Paul told her he wanted was a big yard for their kids to play in. Of course, the house Diane picked out had a yard only slightly bigger than your average phone booth. So instead of hiding that little detail, Diane led with it. "And, honey, the best thing is, you won't be spending all your time sweating behind the lawn mower! You'll have more time to play with the kids."

Game over. They bought the house.

But what if you're trying to persuade someone who's not the love of your life? That's when you need real creativity. The folks at L'Oreal do this when they brag that their hair color is the most expensive on the market. We've all seen the glamorous models running their fingers through their shimmering hair, cooing, "Expensive? Yes. But I'm worth it." All of a sudden, the high price of a hair dye becomes an advantage, a strong point.

Ross Perot tried to do this with his lack of governmental experience. When then President Bush emphasized his vast governmental experience, Perot countered that he was right. Perot agreed he had no experience running up trillions of dollars of debt, no experience plunging the country into a recession, no experience sitting idle as millions of people lost their jobs. Perot used his lack of experience to whip Bush like a borrowed mule.

In 1984 we were working for then–State Senator Lloyd Doggett in his campaign for United States Senate. Doggett was opposed in the Democratic primary by two powerhouse politicians: Kent Hance, a popular congressman from Lubbock who won his seat by defeating an up-and-coming politician named George W. Bush, and Bob Krueger, a former congressman and special ambassador to Mexico. Krueger began to needle Doggett for his lack of experience, suggesting that Doggett's experience in the state senate was hardly the right preparation for the world's greatest deliberative body.

Krueger made a fatal error, though, when he described himself as a "big leaguer" and dismissed Doggett as a "little leaguer." James 'bout jumped through the roof when he heard that. "That's great! That's perfect!" he screamed. Paul couldn't fathom what was so doggone perfect about being mocked like that, but James saw the opening he needed to transform Doggett's weakness—lack of Washington experience—into a strength.

He gave Doggett a baseball bat and a cap and sent him to hold press events in every Little League field where he could draw a camera. From Lubbock to Lufkin, from the Red River to the Rio Grande, "Little League Lloyd" promised to fight for all the Little Leaguers in Texas and against all the big-shot, big-league, big-money special interests in Washington. "We don't need more Washington thinking in Texas," Doggett would say. "We need more Texas thinking in Washington."

On primary day "Little League Lloyd" knocked "Big League Bob" out of the game.

Mom Friday's Chicken Salad

Speaking of making chicken salad, Paul's mother-in-law, Jean Friday, makes the best chicken salad in Austin. (See Rule Two to more fully understand why this recipe's here.)

4 skinless, boneless chicken breast halves
6 cups water
1¼ tsp. salt
2 cups finely chopped red Delicious apple
1 cup chopped celery
1 (2.25-oz.) pkg. sliced almonds, toasted (or you can use chopped pecans)

⅓ cup plain nonfat yogurt
3 tbsp. Low-Fat Miracle Whip Salad Dressing
1 tbsp. honey (optional; it gives the salad a slightly sweeter flavor)
1 tbsp. lemon juice
¼ tsp. pepper

Put the chicken in a large saucepan with the water and 1 tsp. salt; bring to a boil, cover, reduce heat and simmer for about 20 to 30 minutes until done. Cut the chicken into bite-size pieces.

Combine the chicken, apple, celery and almonds in a large bowl. Stir together the remaining ingredients and add to the chicken mixture; toss well. Cover and chill.

Serve on lettuce leaves or in a sandwich.

Yield: 4 to 6 servings

Different People Learn in Different Ways

One of the many reasons a free society is preferable to a totalitarian regime is that we're not consigned by the government to a career path chosen for us at age twelve based on some bureaucrat's idea of the perfect standardized test. But as school reformers from both the left and the right advocate more and more testing, we think it's important to remind the test takers, the test givers and the parents of this very important fact: A person is more than the number stamped on his or her forehead as the result of a standardized test. And no one's potential should ever be limited merely by his or her facility with a number two pencil.

Everyone has a different kind of genius and a different way of learning. Paul was one of those kids who whizzed through those tests as if they were designed for him (which as a middle-class, white, suburban boy, they were). Because of those tests he won a National Merit Scholarship and went to the University of Texas.

James, on the other hand, was a terrible test taker. He struggled in school and dropped out of college. But over time he was able to prove his intelligence and competence in places that were more conducive to his talents. In all his years in politics, no candidate has ever asked him what he scored on the college boards. Nor has anyone ever said, "We'd like to hire you for our campaign, James. But could you first take this test. Just fill in the appropriate bubbles with a number two pencil. We'll be back to grade it in two hours."

Just because your genius is not the kind that Brown or Princeton immediately recognizes doesn't mean you have to be relegated to a second-class life. You may have to work harder, you may have to fight the system a little more, but if you're persistent, you'll have a chance to go to college and show your wares. And the deeper you get into the real world, the less your SAT scores or even where you went to college matter. James has lectured all over the world and never tires of reminding his audience of his poor scholastic performance.

In fact, people who are forced to succeed despite having

nontraditional kinds of intelligence often develop better work habits and sterner characters than folks who excel in the traditional way. We're convinced that everyone deserves a venue to prove themselves.

A woman named Sally Smith in Washington has made a career out of proving that very point. She is the mother of a child with severe learning disabilities. In 1967 she came to realize that the schools in the Washington area—both public and private—were ill equipped to teach kids who learned differently from others. But she didn't quit and she didn't succumb to the notion that her kid was not smart.

She started her own school.

Sally's school, the Lab School of Washington, is a monument to a mother's love and to the Jeffersonian concept that all Americans should have access to opportunity. Rather than a crummy facility for supposedly "crummy" students, the Lab School sits on a campus that could house a college.

The Lab School works miracles. Kids who a generation ago would have been written off now are challenged and stimulated and encouraged—and taught. Ninety percent of the high school students go on to college.

The lesson is simple: Don't think that a deficiency in one area is a life sentence. Maximize your strengths, minimize your weaknesses and find a way to succeed.

Be Honest in Your Self-Assessment

In order to maximize your strengths and minimize your weaknesses, or to turn your weaknesses into strengths, you've first got to be able to identify them and distinguish one from the other. If you're not brutally honest in your self-assessment, you're going to waste a lot of time down the road.

One of our favorite stories that illustrates this principle is the one about a kid who tried to walk onto a football team. (Paul tells this story using the Texas Longhorns; James the LSU Tigers. Feel free to substitute the team of your choice.) The kid marches up to the coach and says, "Coach, you've got to put me on the team. I can throw a football in a perfect spiral right through a tire hanging from the goalpost from 70 yards away. Not only that, I can run the 40-yard dash in four seconds flat. And what's more, I didn't miss a field goal from inside the 50-yard line in all four years of high school."

The coach looks at the boy in amazement, then skepticism. "Come on, son," he says. "Every athlete has his drawbacks. It's fine that you can do all those things. But what's the weakest part of your game?"

"I can't think of anything, Coach," the boy says. "Except I do tend to exaggerate."

Be honest with yourself and others. Try to choose a path that exposes your shortcomings as little as possible and accentuates your strengths as much as possible. This may sound like common sense because it is. But common sense is not too common in this life. Most people don't take the path that best suits their talents. They take the path that most other people take. So do lemmings, and they wind up marching off cliffs.

So don't be a lemming. If your strengths lead you on an untraditional path, so be it. Celebrate your choice. Read Robert Frost's "The Road Not Taken" and contemplate whether you're better suited for the road less traveled.

"My Way or the Highway" Is Dead-End Leadership

A good leader understands that everyone learns differently. A bad leader thinks everyone should learn the way he or she does. The "my way or the highway" style of leadership is a thing of the past. Those who practice it are going to get whipped every time they compete against an organization that develops talent in every way it can.

Mort Meyerson is one of the great geniuses of the technology industry. Along with that little Martian Ross Perot, he founded EDS and built it into one of the powerhouses of the information age. Under Perot and Meyerson EDS had a rigid, quasi-military culture that emphasized values like hard work, quality and consistency. But it also created a climate that some of the more creative folks there found stultifying. All of the men had to keep their hair short and wear dark suits, long-sleeved white shirts and ties. Women could not wear miniskirts or flat shoes; they could not wear their hair too long or their eye shadow too heavy. Alcohol was not allowed at company functions, and marital infidelity was a firing offense. No facial hair was allowed on men; no pants were allowed on women. (We can't find any prohibition on bearded women or skirts on men, so maybe EDS was more progressive than we're giving them credit for.)[1]

Max Hopper, one of EDS's bright young prospects, bristled at the strictures and structure. Although he was clearly gifted, he just didn't fit into the EDS corporate culture. And the company's inflexible, one-size-fits-all style of leadership ultimately drove him off.

Once freed from the EDS straitjacket, Hopper devised the SABRE program, which is the state-of-the-art software for all airline reservations. He made a fortune for himself and his investors, a fortune EDS would have reaped if only it had known how to develop nontraditional talent.

Years later, reflecting on the lessons he'd learned from a long and successful career, Meyerson acknowledged that the suffocating corporate culture had been a mistake. He wished he'd been more open to people who learned differently. In 1996 Meyerson wrote an article in *Fast Company,* which he titled "Everything I Thought I Knew About Leadership Is Wrong." In it he admits: "Looking back on the boot camp mentality that we used to shape leaders, I see how quick I was to judge others. Today I believe that leaders need to be good at psychology—starting with self-knowledge."[2]

In a photograph accompanying the article, Meyerson was wearing a beard.

If everyone looked, thought and acted the same, the world would look like an Osmond family Christmas special. Truth is, the world—and the workplace—looks a lot more like the United Nations General Assembly than the Osmond family. Different people, different talents, different perspectives, different strengths—and weaknesses. Effective leadership requires a level of creativity that would have been unheard of just a generation ago. That means seeking out previously untapped talent, challenging people and channeling attributes that are a weakness in one field into an area where they become a strength.

Bill Clinton loved to say, "We don't have a person to waste." He was right. Whether you're competing in a campaign or a corporation, you can't afford to carry dead weight. If you're imaginative and flexible, who knows, you may even transform a jumpy, unfocused kid with a report card full of F's and a disrespectful smart-ass into relatively productive people.

Be Nimble, Jack

VON Clausewitz called it "friction."

The legendary military strategist was referring to his earlier, Teutonic version of Murphy's Law. When a battle plan is made, it invariably contains certain assumptions. Assumptions about the weather, or the size and capability of forces, or the contours of the terrain, or the capacity of matériel. When a real battle is engaged in the real world, things change. Events don't ever come to pass exactly as we expect them to. When "the fog of war" (another von Clausewitz phrase) sets in, things don't look as clear as when they were planned.

This is all just a fancy way of saying: Shit happens.

Recognizing this reality is one of the keys to success. The ability to adapt to a changing environment, to adjust to new realities, is essential.

Intentional Versus Improvisational

In analyzing the presidency, we've come to believe that there are in fact two presidencies: the intentional presidency and the improvisational presidency. The intentional presidency consists of the ideas and issues the president campaigned on and claims a mandate for. For Reagan it was cutting taxes and opposing Communism. For Clinton it was reviving the economy, reforming welfare and reducing crime. Both presidents are considered successful, but not merely because they fulfilled their core campaign promises. No, they're considered successful because they mastered the improvisational presidency.

Three months into his term, on March 30, 1981, Ronald Reagan was shot and nearly killed. Hemingway defined courage as "grace under pressure" and Reagan showed amazing grace. As he lay bleeding in the hospital, he delivered to his wife, Nancy, a line from an old movie: "Honey, I forgot to duck." John Hinckley's bullet only missed the Gipper's heart by inches, and we now know that Reagan was far more grievously wounded than we were told at the time. Four months later 13,000 members of the Professional Air Traffic Controllers went on strike. Although he was a former union president himself, Reagan gave the air traffic controllers forty-eight hours to return to work and then fired all who didn't.

Clinton, too, showed that he could master the unexpected. His amazing ability to survive scandal and stumbles to defeat an incumbent president who had scored the highest popularity ratings in history was one thing—but at least it was based on a strategy. He had no idea that his presidency would be defined in part by how he handled losing the Congress to the Gingrich revolutionaries, how he brought hope and healing to the nation after the Oklahoma City bombing and how he outfoxed the Republicans to win the showdown over the government shutdown.

Both presidents were master improvisers. They adapted

to changing circumstances. Reagan the tax cutter actually signed into law the Tax Equity and Fiscal Responsibility Act of 1982, a mouthful of words that means: big-ass tax increase. As the *Wall Street Journal* reported: "Contrary to Republican claims, the 1993 (Clinton) package . . . is not 'the largest tax increase in history.' The 1982 deficit reduction package of President Reagan and Sen. Robert Dole in a GOP-controlled Senate was a bigger tax bill, both in 1993 adjusted dollars and as a percentage of the overall economy. . . ."[1] Clinton showed he could adapt as well. In 1996 he signed a welfare reform bill that was much closer to the Republicans' principles than to those he'd articulated during the 1992 campaign.

Were they hypocrites? No, not really. Just leaders who were flexible enough to change with the times.

Same goes for your career. We all have two careers: the career we seek, plan for and try to create and the unintentional, unplanned career. And our improvisational career is usually more exciting, more challenging and more rewarding than our intentional career—if we have the ability to adjust, adapt and enjoy the roller coaster.

"Well, God, I Guess You're Testing Me"

Being flexible allows you to handle whatever comes your way. In 1993 President Clinton traveled to Capitol Hill to address a joint session of Congress to introduce his health care plan. In typical Clinton fashion we'd labored on the speech up until the last minute. As Clinton took the rostrum in the House Chamber, he turned around and said to Vice President Gore, "Al, look at the TelePromTer. They've got the wrong speech up there."

Sure enough, the speech on the TelePrompTer was the speech he'd given months ago, in support of his economic plan. He had a paper printout of the correct speech, but the type was too small for him to see without his glasses, which he didn't have.

Holy shit.

Gore told George Stephanopoulos, who, along with the brilliant Clinton communications aide David Dreyer, frantically tried to load the correct speech into the machine. But before they could fix the problem, the applause died down. Congress—and the nationwide TV audience—was ready to hear the speech.

Of course, Clinton improvised. He riffed. He knew the policy and the politics so intimately that the stuff he made up was as good or better than the text we'd spent weeks preparing. All this while the wrong speech was furiously whizzing up and down, backwards and forwards, on the screen in front of his face—in a desperate effort to find the right speech.

After an interminable nine minutes, Dreyer finally saved

the day. He'd loaded a backup copy of the speech on his laptop and transferred it to the TelePrompTer. And when he saw the correct speech coming up on the screen, Clinton seamlessly transferred to the prepared text.

After the speech, Paul and Dreyer approached Clinton to apologize and take full responsibility for the foul-up. (See Rule Eleven to understand the wisdom of accepting responsibility even when the screwup isn't yours.) But Clinton was ebullient and forgiving. Later that night Paul pulled Clinton aside. "I've got to know, Mr. President," he said. "When you were standing up there without the speech, what was going through your mind?"

Clinton smiled, draped his arm around Paul and said, "I thought, 'Well, God, you're testing me. Okay. Here goes.' Then I just took a deep breath and launched into it."

Maybe Nixon Really Was the One

As good as Reagan and Clinton were at adapting, Richard Milhous Nixon was one of the most brilliantly flexible politicians we've ever seen. Consider how his career began. He came into politics as a red-baiting right-winger, serving as one of Joe McCarthy's young allies in the House of Representatives. From his perch on the House Un-American Activities Committee (the very name itself conjures up images of a twentieth-century Spanish Inquisition), Nixon railed relentlessly against Communists, which he alleged were infiltrating our government.

He made his name by going after Alger Hiss, an Ivy League diplomat with an aristocratic bent. He accused Hiss of being a spy, a charge Nixon was never able to prove in court. Still, Hiss was convicted of perjury—lying in Nixon's hearing when he denied ever having been a Communist.

On the heels of his triumph over Hiss, Nixon sought a seat in the United States Senate. He got it the same way he got Hiss: by red-baiting. He called his opponent, a decent and loyal American named Helen Gahagan Douglas, "pink right down to her underwear." The charge was absurd, it was sexist—and it was effective.

It's hard to believe that the same man who gloried in hunting down Hiss and smearing Douglas would achieve his greatest legacy by embracing some of the most murderous Communists in history. And yet Richard Nixon was nimble enough to respond to the overtures of Chinese leader Mao Tse-tung and recognize the largest, reddest nation on earth, declaring, "There is no place on this small planet for a billion of its potentially most able people to live in angry isolation."

He began with "Ping-Pong" diplomacy—using sports to break the ice. Then he sent his secretary of state, Henry Kissinger, to China to cut a deal that would have meant eternal hostility from the right if it had been negotiated by anyone other than Nixon. The United States—and President Nixon—would withdraw its troops from Taiwan (the island from which the most fervent anti-Communists hoped to retake mainland China) and end its opposition to seating the People's Republic of China at the United Nations. This would mean that Taiwan would be expelled from the UN. By 1972 Nixon became the first American president to visit Communist China, where he and Chairman Mao were pictured clinking champagne glasses and signing the Shanghai Communiqué, which recognized Communist China as the one and only China (as opposed to Taiwan).[2]

The old Commie fighter also worked to thaw relations

with the Soviet Union, becoming the first president to visit the USSR as well, toasting the savage Soviet leader Leonid Brezhnev and establishing a policy of "détente" with the Soviets, the crowning achievement of which was the U.S./Soviet Strategic Arms Limitation Treaty (SALT I).[3]

Of course, Nixon did not set out on a careful, lifelong strategy first to establish his bona fides as a virulent anti-Communist so that, decades later, as president he could achieve a rapprochement with China and the USSR. Rather, Nixon was dexterous. Whether it was finding Communists under every bed in Washington in the 1950s or signing treaties with real Communists in the 1970s, Nixon was the consummate opportunist.

How else can you explain the man's remarkable career? He was not the beneficiary of an elite education or the scion of a wealthy family. Far from it, he was raised in gritty poverty in Yorba Linda, California, and educated at Whittier College. Physically he was ugly; socially he was awkward.

But politically he was as flexible as Baryshnikov.

After a narrow defeat in the presidential election of 1960, Nixon flopped again in the California governor's race in 1962. After losing that race he dramatically withdrew from politics and told a press conference, "You won't have Nixon to kick around anymore."

But Flexible Dick didn't mean it. He carefully remade his image and by 1968 was running as "the New Nixon" in much the same way that laundry detergents periodically declare themselves "New and Improved." It worked. He won a narrow victory in a three-way race, defeating both Vice President Hubert Humphrey and Alabama governor George Wallace (who was running as an anti-integration independent).

Nixon was a study in contradiction. He had no history of

racial animus, yet was elected president in part because of a "southern strategy" that played upon southern white fears and resentments that had been stirred up by Wallace. He was a pro-business Republican, yet he signed into law legislation creating the Environmental Protection Agency and the Occupational Health and Safety Administration. As a young congressman he had voted to repeal the wartime wage and price controls; as president he placed new government controls on wages and prices. He was from the party's conservative wing, yet he chose a former Kennedy and Johnson aide, Daniel Patrick Moynihan, to advise him on domestic policy. As he campaigned for the presidency in 1968, he promised to "Bring us together." And yet he proved to be one of the most divisive presidents in history.

Keep Learning

Nixon succeeded, albeit temporarily, because he rode the currents of swiftly changing times. There are no riots in the streets today. But politicians can still find themselves out of step with the times.

"Lifelong learning" is one of those buzzwords that education-reform weenies throw around—for good reason. Gone are the days when people could learn all they needed to know in twelve or sixteen or even twenty years of formal schooling. The world today is dynamic; times change, knowledge expands. A big part of being nimble is constantly educating yourself, challenging assumptions, examining orthodoxies.

As Benjamin Disraeli once said, "A good leader knows himself and the times." By that standard, Roy Barnes is a good leader. Barnes was the brightest star of the "courthouse conservatives" in Georgia, the rural Democrats who'd run the state ever since Reconstruction ended. Barnes had a charm and a wit and a brain that had made him one of the most respected, popular and effective state senators in Georgia. He ran for governor in 1990 as the candidate of the old, established order. And like the old guard, Barnes wasn't big on change. He opposed the notion of a Georgia lottery and bragged that he'd never seen the Pacific Ocean, never even been west of the Rockies. In the old days guys like Roy Barnes won the Democratic primary easily, then coasted to victory in the November election.

But Georgia was changing and Barnes hadn't changed with it. He placed third in a field of four candidates. Barnes lost to Zell Miller, another product of the old county-courthouse system. But with the help of the two best southern strategists we've ever seen, Keith Mason and Steve Wrigley, Miller sensed the shifting terrain and moved with it. Miller, who was once chief of staff to the segregationist governor Lester Maddox, reinvented himself as a suburban moderate with a signature issue: universal college scholarships financed by a lottery. We worked for Miller in that election, and it was one of the best experiences of our lives.

After losing to Miller, Barnes returned to the state legislature—this time as a lowly state representative. He licked his wounds and studied his state. He saw that the rural domination of Georgia was over. For all its southern charm, Georgia had become a thoroughly suburban state. So Barnes changed with the times. He roared back into the limelight in 1998, running as a pro-reform, pro-education, suburban pol. He had a plan for growth management, a plan for transportation to ease the nightmare of the suburban Atlanta commute, plans for cleaner water and more green space. And his signature issue was the quintessentially New Democrat cause: patients' rights. "If you can choose who changes the oil in your car," he said in his ads, "you ought to be able to choose who delivers your baby."

Barnes won a decisive victory in 1998. As governor he's traveled to Japan, Israel, Europe and Canada to promote a twenty-first century Georgia that engages with the world. He's passed his patients' rights bill, as well as an innovative tax incentive to encourage on-site child-care centers for corporations.

Barnes didn't flip-flop, didn't abandon his ideals. But he did change with the times. The man who was once the model good ol' boy is now the archetypal modern southern governor.

The Greatest

It's one of the great barroom debates of all time, but if we had to lay a dollar on the table and bet on who the greatest boxer of all time was we wouldn't have to think twice: Muhammad Ali.

Ali had it all: brains, looks, athleticism, wit, marketing savvy and the killer instinct it takes to be a champion. But even more remarkable than all of his God-given talent was Ali's ability to redefine and reinvent himself in the ring and in life itself.

When he fought Sonny Liston for the heavyweight championship of the world in 1964, only three out of the forty-six sportswriters gathered to cover the fight predicted Cassius Clay (as Ali was then known) would win. He was an 8-to-1 underdog dismissed as "the Louisville Lip," while Liston was a brooding, hulking, lethal bear of a man who had destroyed Floyd Patterson and was rumored to be connected to the Mob. But Clay brashly predicted that he would win in eight rounds.

Clay took command of the fight immediately. His combination of speed and power seemed to confuse and anger Liston, who lunged wildly at his fast-moving target. Clay defied all boxing conventions by avoiding Liston's punches simply by leaning back rather than doing the classic bob-and-weave. He seemed to be cruising to victory.

But in the fourth round Clay's eyes widened as he jerked his head back from a Liston punch. In the brief rest between rounds, Clay told his trainer, Angelo Dundee, that something was in his eyes. They were burning and he couldn't see. Must have been something from Liston's glove, some foreign substance. Clay asked Dundee to cut his gloves off and stop the fight. Dundee pushed the blinded Clay back into the ring with this brilliant advice: "Stay away from him. Stay away."

Thanks, Angelo.

Can you imagine the terror, the confusion, the frustration of being a twenty-two-year-old in the fight of your life against a menacing opponent, on the verge of accomplishing your life's dream when all of a sudden you can't see? Clay had to think fast. He had to adapt. He obviously couldn't continue to stick and move as he had so successfully for four rounds.

Detecting his opponent's confusion, Liston charged like a wounded bull. He nailed Clay again and again with punishing shots to the body. Clay, blinking furiously to clear his eyes, danced as fast as he could, circling the ring, trying to keep his distance from Liston's lethal left hook. Clay frequently put his left hand on Liston's head, trying to keep him at bay with his superior reach. Clay was fighting by Braille.

By the sixth round Clay's eyes had cleared, and he put Liston away, winning by a technical knockout. Cassius Clay's brilliant improvising had made him the heavyweight champion of the world.

After the fight, Clay made an even more astonishing transformation. The out-of-control wild-man braggart of the prefight hysteria was suddenly a subdued, soft-spoken champion. In the postfight press conference, reporters even had to call out to him, "Speak louder, Cassius. We can't hear you." Wearing a respectable gray tweed sports coat, Cassius Clay announced, "I'm through talking. All I have to be is a nice, clean gentleman."

Then that nice, clean gentleman shocked the world for a second time. He announced that he was a Muslim, a follower of the controversial Nation of Islam leader Elijah Muhammad and his charismatic spokesman, Malcolm X.

He was stripped of his title for refusing to serve in the army (memorably telling the world, "I ain't got no quarrel with them Vietcong"). The boastful clown was now a serious worldwide symbol. Ali became the flashpoint for everything controversial in the '60s: the Vietnam War, racial tensions and youthful rebellion.

Ali's ability to reinvent himself in the ring allowed him to come back from a three-year layoff and win two out of three classic fights against Joe Frazier, but it was in his title bout against George Foreman in Kinshasa, Zaire, that Ali sealed his legacy as the greatest improviser—as well as the greatest fighter—ever to step into the ring.

No one knowledgeable about boxing, probably not even Ali's cornermen, truly believed the aging Ali could defeat the young, hard-hitting Foreman, who was 40–0 with twenty-four knockouts in a row.

Round after round Foreman rained furious blows down

on Ali, who leaned against the ropes, pathetically trying to protect himself and rarely hitting back. But by the end of the fourth round Foreman's legs were weary. The young bull was tired. His arms were heavy. He began lunging at Ali, punching with his body as much as his mighty fists. But he kept pouring it on—and Ali kept taking it.

It was becoming apparent that there was a method to Ali's madness. The "rope-a-dope" strategy was causing Foreman to punch himself out, while Ali conserved his strength in the African heat. But, just as in the Liston fight a decade earlier, something happened that forced Ali to modify a strategy that had been working perfectly.

During the intermission between rounds five and six, a Zairian official who was trying to tighten the top rope inadvertently loosened it. If Ali leaned against the ropes now, he'd likely fall over into the crowd.

Once more the master improviser had to think on the run—and not just on the run but while he was being pounded by one of the most fearsome fighters in boxing history. So Ali changed tactics once again, spending rounds six and seven punishing Foreman's face with jabs, all the while trying to keep his distance from the knockout punch that Foreman was trying to unload.

Then, in round eight, the final tactic. Ali unleashed a withering left-right combination, out-power-punching the most powerful puncher on earth. Exhausted and punched out, Foreman was unable to defend himself; he crashed to the African canvas.

Muhammad Ali became the first man to win the heavyweight championship of the world three different times: once as a dancing, prancing young stud against Sonny Liston, later going toe-to-toe in a legendary slugfest with Joe Frazier and finally outfoxing and outboxing George Foreman.

In his postfight career Ali has proved as adaptable as ever. His nearly perfect body is ravaged with Parkinson's, his loud, proud voice now virtually silent. The brash young radical is now an elder statesman. But he was then, is now and always will be The Greatest.

The lesson here is that the battle does not always go to the biggest or the strongest. Especially in a fast-paced, ever-changing environment, the winner is going to be the person with the greatest ability to adapt. It's no surprise that the only two-term presidents in the last forty years (Nixon, Reagan and Clinton) were all masters of flexibility, able to reinvent themselves as circumstances changed. Flexibility confounds and confuses your adversaries and builds a sense of self-confidence that you can handle anything they throw at you.

There Is Such a Thing as Being *Too* Flexible

A brief caveat as we praise flexibility: On matters of basic principle, elasticity can make you a hollow man. Case in point: George Corley Wallace.

As evidenced by the remarkable footage collected in the stunning documentary *Settin' the Woods on Fire*, George Wallace started his political career as a liberal—and an integrationist.

Wallace won his first election—for the Alabama legislature—in 1946. He became known as a populist politician who was generous in his dealings with black Alabamians. In 1948 he refused to join in as his colleagues in the Alabama delegation to the Democratic National Convention walked out in protest over the party's new pro–civil rights stance. In 1949 he sought and received an appointment to the Board of Trustees of the Tuskegee Institute, which was founded by Booker T. Washington to educate African Americans.

Wallace continued to distinguish himself as a racial progressive while serving as a state judge from 1953 to 1958. The African American attorney J. L. Chestnut describes Wallace in *Settin' the Woods on Fire* as "the most liberal judge I ever practiced law in front of."

In 1958 he ran for governor. In the Democratic primary (which in Alabama in those days was tantamount to the election, since there was no real Republican Party), Wallace courageously attacked the Ku Klux Klan and refused its support. He received and accepted the support of the NAACP, which the state of Alabama had outlawed two years earlier.

He told audiences on the campaign trail, "I want to tell the good people of this state, as a judge of the third judicial circuit, if I didn't have what it takes to treat a man fair, regardless of his color, then I don't have what it takes to be the governor of your great state." He declared categorically: "I advocate hatred of no man, because hate will only compound the problems facing the South."

Wallace was soundly defeated by pro-KKK candidate John Patterson. He tells Seymore Trammell, his finance director, "I was out-niggered and I will never be out-niggered again."

Indeed, just seven months after his defeat. Wallace pronounced himself a hard-line segregationist. He refused to cooperate with the U.S. Civil Rights Commission's investigation into voting rights abuses, risking a jail term for failing to turn over records under his control as a judge. (He ultimately handed them over and stayed out of jail, but the ploy firmly established his nascent segregationist credentials.)

The rest is a sad and sorry history. In 1961 Wallace named his daughter after Robert E. Lee. In 1962 he was elected in a landslide on an anti-integration platform and declared in his infamous inaugural: "It is very appropriate that from this cradle of the Confederacy, this very heart of the great Anglo-Saxon Southland, that today we sound the drum for freedom as have our generations of forebears before us time and again down through history. Let us rise to the call for freedom-loving blood that is in us and send our answer to the tyranny that clanks its chains upon the South. In the name of the greatest people who have ever trod this earth, I draw the line in the dust and toss the gauntlet before the feet of tyranny, and I say segregation now, segregation tomorrow, segregation forever."

Wallace stood in the schoolhouse door to oppose integration of the University of Alabama, dispatched state troopers who beat John Lewis and other heroes nearly to death as they tried to march across the Edmund Pettus Bridge in Selma, Alabama.

He ran for president in 1964, 1968, 1972 and 1976, always bashing the federal government, the engine of racial integration.

Toward the end of his life he sought and received the forgiveness of such civil rights heroes as John Lewis and the Reverend Jesse Jackson. But some saw this as just another cynical move for political expediency. And, indeed, Wallace won a fourth and final term as governor in 1982 in part on his strong support from African Americans.

Would we respect Wallace more if he'd been like Byron de la Beckwith, the monster who murdered Medgar Evers, who thought African Americans were not fully human? No. But Wallace compounded the evil of racism with the evil of political cynicism, pitting Americans against one another, inciting violence and helping to plunge his region and our nation into its most painful and divisive period since the Civil War.[4]

Rule 11

Know How to Recover When You *Really* Screw Up

LET'S face it: everybody screws up. There's not a one of us who hasn't. The difference for politicians is that their screwups wind up on the front page of the paper. So politicians—good ones at least—develop an ability to recover from a foul-up. Fortunately or not, we've become exquisitely experienced in disaster management. Here's what we've learned from our sometimes painful experience.

'Fess Up

This runs contrary to human nature and is much easier said than done. But if you 'fess up you're taking responsibility, thereby demonstrating that even when you mess up you're responsible. Besides, accepting responsibility sounds better, feels better—hell, it *is* better—than accepting blame. Blame is something others assign to you. Blame bad; responsibility good.

One of the most dramatic and effective examples of taking responsibility we know of was when Bill Hobby was the lieutenant governor of Texas. On June 20, 1974, Hobby was arrested at 2:48 A.M. by the Austin Police Department. He was drunk, he was driving, and he was with a woman who was not his wife. The police said that Hobby's car had been weaving dangerously across the center line; that when Hobby was pulled over, he got out of his car and stumbled; that he smelled strongly of alcohol, had bloodshot eyes, staggered when he walked and refused to take a Breathalyzer test. When police searched the car they found an empty one-gallon bottle of wine and a fifth of Cutty Sark scotch, two-thirds of which had apparently been guzzled.

To fully comprehend the impact of this foul-up, you've got to understand more about Bill Hobby and Texas. Bill Hobby's father was a legendary governor of Texas from 1917 to 1921. His mother, Oveta Culp Hobby, was the first secretary of Health, Education and Welfare and the first commanding officer of the WAC, the Women's Army Corps. The Hobbys also were among the most successful businesspeople in Texas, owning the *Houston Post* as well as radio and television properties. Bill Hobby was Texas royalty.

Not only that, he was lieutenant governor of Texas. Unlike most states, where the job description of the lieutenant governor is to check periodically on the health of the governor, the lieutenant governor is the most powerful person in state government. The lieutenant governor appoints every chairman and every member of every committee in the state senate, over which he presides and through which little or no legislation passes without his approval.

In addition to this stranglehold over the legislative branch, the lieutenant governor also has broad control over the executive branch of government. Texas has a weak governor system, to say the least. Rather than a cabinet form of government, with each agency head hired by the governor, Texas has a commission form of government. The governor can nominate members of those commissions, but they must be approved by the state senate (that is, the lieutenant governor's state senate), and once approved, commission members cannot be fired by the governor for anything less than serious corruption (mild corruption being a Texas tradition that rivals high school football). But those commissions' budgets are largely written by—you guessed it—the lieutenant governor, giving him enormous leverage over every aspect of state government.

As lieutenant governors go, Bill Hobby was the best. He was exceedingly knowledgeable about state government, considering how it was a family business and all. And unlike some scions of powerful families, Hobby was secure, pleasant to be around and had no chip on his shoulder. So when he screwed up, it was a B-I-G story.

Hobby called his lawyer, who bailed him out of jail in the middle of the night. He went home, cleaned up and, with his wife in tow, went out to face the media. He told the assembled mob he was guilty. He apologized for his actions, saying he was "extremely sorry" and asked citizens to judge him "on the basis of all [his] actions." Hobby pleaded no contest to the drunk-driving charge and accepted humbly the punishment the court handed down.

Mrs. Hobby, while refusing public comment, spoke volumes when she appeared with her husband in court, smiling at reporters and strategically—and purposefully—

positioning herself so that her head was over his shoulder as he spoke to the press and would therefore be in the TV picture. The young woman was never heard from again.

End of story.

The Hobby strategy worked because even a pack of dogs stops pursuing you when you stop. Sometimes, with dogs, they rip the flesh off your bones, but political animals are different. What more could they do to Hobby that he hadn't already done to himself? What more could they say about him that he hadn't already said himself? What were his opponents going to do—accuse him of drunk driving and being in the presence of a woman who was not his wife late at night? Duh.

In fact, while Hobby's political opponents initially tried to make political hay out of the drunk-driving incident, the tactic failed. One politico said, "It's going to come back to haunt him. It's not going to be forgotten—if his opponents don't bring it up, the newspapers will."

But the newspapers were so disarmed by Hobby's candor that they actually praised him. "With the exception of an occasional dyspeptic letter to the editor, the Hobby affair is a thing of the past," wrote the editor of the Corpus Christi *Caller Times* just two weeks after Hobby's arrest. "The reason, of course, was that the lieutenant governor did nothing that could prolong the public's curiosity about his offense. He did not contest the arresting officer's charges. He made no alibis. He took his medicine from the judge. . . . It was smart—but it still took a lot of guts."

The *San Antonio Express-News* opined, "Hobby has set a rare example for a high public official. He was caught in an embarrassing and compromising episode and he never tried to cover it up. . . . We can recall other high officials who failed their candor test under similar circumstances."

The *Austin American-Statesman* fairly gushed: "Lt. Gov.

Bill Hobby was only the latest in a long line of Texas public officials who have been arrested for driving under the influence of alcohol. So far as the record shows, Bill Hobby is the only one of those to stand up like a man and admit his misdeed and take his medicine. . . . His was a human error not unknown to many Texans. The stamp of character is in the manner he chose to bear the consequences unflinchingly and with due contrition."

Perhaps cowed by the coverage, Hobby's Republican opponent backed off from his initial criticism of Hobby, mewing, "I certainly will not cause this to be a campaign issue. What a man does in his personal life is personal. I feel bad any time someone is in a situation like that."

Fundamentalists, on the other hand, were already angered over Hobby's support for legalizing horse racing. They pounced. "A lot of people were disappointed in his stand on gambling," said Phil Strickland of the Christian Life Commission of the Baptist General Convention of Texas. "Add this on top of that and there is going to be some folks who are not going to be voting for him."

Apparently Brother Strickland's political prognosticating is as bad as his grammar.

Hobby went on to be reelected in November of 1974, a little over four months after his arrest. He was reelected again and again, served for eighteen years and is widely regarded as the finest lieutenant governor in Texas history. A major state office building in Austin proudly bears his name, just a few miles from where he was arrested.

Take Away Their Spears

One of the most gifted advance men we ever worked with was a young man named Andrew Beaver. After much success in politics, Andrew became a gay rights activist, one of the early members of the group Queer Nation. We asked Andrew why a gay rights group would give itself such an offensive name. He said, "We want to take the spears away from our oppressors. We've already declared that we're queer. Maybe that can get us beyond the name calling and allow us to talk about how gay people are treated in this country."

The actor Ben Jones effectively utilized this technique when he ran for Congress from Georgia. He was best known as Cooter in the hit TV series *The Dukes of Hazzard,* but the press and his opponents soon seized on his personal life. It seems ol' Cooter had a fondness for the bottle and the ladies. Instead of hiding out, Ben 'fessed up, declaring, "It's true. I used to spend ninety percent of my money on whiskey and women. The other ten percent I just wasted."

Ben won his race for Congress.

Set Things Right

Oftentimes simply fessing up isn't enough. You've got to take steps to set right what you've done wrong.

On Sunday, September 28, 1980, the *Washington Post* published a story called "Jimmy's World" by Janet Cooke on its front page. The story was about an eight-year-old heroin addict in the District of Columbia who was being mistreated and was essentially being treated like a prisoner by his mother and her boyfriend. The story was said to be based on interviews with the boy, his mother and his mother's boyfriend.

Cooke had told her editors before the article's publication that she was able to get access to Jimmy because she had promised his family anonymity. She also said that the mother's boyfriend had warned her against bringing in police authorities and had threatened her personally. Cooke's immediate supervisor, the *Post*'s city editor, agreed to run the story while protecting the confidentiality of her sources.

The story created an immediate uproar. People were outraged when the *Post* refused to reveal Jimmy's name or address so the authorities could help the boy. Washington police chief Burtell Jefferson launched a citywide search. Schools, social services and police contacts were asked to help locate Jimmy. The police search continued for seventeen days but turned up nothing.

Some in the *Post* newsroom were beginning to doubt Jimmy's existence, but one of the people who had authority over the piece was none other than Bob Woodward, then the metro editor of the *Post* and its brightest star, the hero of Watergate. Woodward had been played by Robert Redford in the film version of *All the President's Men*. His personal endorsement of "Jimmy's World" carried enormous weight.

Woodward attributed the skepticism to "professional jealousy," and the story was submitted, with Woodward's strong support, to the Pulitzer Prize Committee.

In the spring of 1981, the story was chosen for the Pulitzer Prize. But within hours discrepancies in Cooke's curriculum vitae (she said she'd graduated with honors from Vassar when in fact she'd only attended Vassar her freshman year and received her B.A. from the University of Toledo) led to questions about the accuracy of her Pulitzer-winning story.

After intense questioning from Woodward and other *Post* editors, Cooke admitted that she'd fabricated the story. She resigned from the paper, and the *Post* ran a Sunday story detailing how she'd invented Jimmy and his world.

Woodward offered to resign from the paper, perhaps knowing that if he went his bosses would have to go, too. Still, it was an honorable gesture. Reflecting on it later in an interview in *Playboy,* Woodward said, "My failure was not only journalistic but moral. I said 'This is a great story' and never looked at the human impact on an eight-year-old. I think my greatest failure when Cooke came in with this story was not to have said 'We're going to run the story tomorrow and then I'm going down to a phone booth and drop a dime myself to the cops and tell them "Go to this address and rescue this child." '

"That might have set off alarm bells to solve the journalistic problem," Woodward continued. "After the story came out, the mayor, to his credit, wanted to know who the child was and where he was. And we took a 'principled' stand, saying, 'No, we have a source relationship with the mother.' Well, that's absurd. It was murder, or slow torture, of a child. If that happened now, I'd think of journalism second and the child first."

Cynics may say that Woodward engaged in a little post-disaster CYA spin. They note that in discussing the matter Woodward liberally sprinkles the names of other editors who dropped the ball before it got to him. But the facts are that he was responsible for the debacle, and he took responsibility for it.

What more could he do? What more could the *Post*'s critics say? Your authors are probably not the paper's biggest fans (we think the *Post* made a fool of itself in the way it hounded and harassed Bill Clinton over Whitewater, Lewinsky and a host of other imagined "scandals," and is now embarrassing itself even more with its fawning coverage of George W), but we frankly admire the way Woodward handled the Janet Cooke debacle.

Credibility is the coin of the realm of journalism. The *Post*'s credibility had been badly damaged by the Janet Cooke scandal. But the best way to rebuild it was to do exactly what Woodward did: He 'fessed up, accepted responsibility and took steps to right the wrong, including eating a giant helping of crow on the front page of his own newspaper.

Fight Back

Now that we've examined case studies of coming clean, then following a disclosure with concrete steps to right the wrong, there's a third tactic that is sometimes called for: the counterattack.

We want to stress the word *sometimes*. Not *often*. And certainly not *always*. Sometimes. Seldom. Occasionally. And only, only after you've already 'fessed up and taken steps to set things right. It's hard to be credible and effective in an attack if you haven't first done effective damage control. But sometimes you have no choice. The Bridgestone/Firestone Company recently executed this difficult maneuver as well as we've ever seen.

As you doubtless recall, Firestone tires were found to be defective. Because of problems of tread separation, Firestone tires were literally coming apart at the seams—and with them the company's century-old reputation for quality, safety and reliability.

After a period of denial, the company ultimately settled on a much smarter strategy, with the aid of Jeff Eller, a War Room veteran turned corporate PR genius. With Eller's help, the company admitted defects in its tires, aided in a government-supervised recall and replaced 6.5 million tires at its own expense. The company also replaced its CEO and made new CEO John Lampe the poster boy for its quality-control turnaround effort.

But even 'fessing up and trying to set things right didn't stop the hemorrhaging. Firestone came to believe that the Ford Motor Company, its customer of nearly one hundred years, was unfairly blaming Firestone tires for what Firestone believed were design flaws in Ford's popular Explorer.

Firestone's very survival as a company was at stake. The lawsuits, the government investigations and the bad publicity were nearly fatal, but there was nothing that could be done to stop them, given the unpleasant fact that the tires truly did have a tread-separation problem.

The *New York Times* had called Firestone asking for a comment on a report that Ford was going to ask for further Firestone recalls. Firestone executives probably felt that if this was how they were going to learn about more problems in their one-hundred-year-old relationship with Ford, the relationship was already over for all practical purposes. Firestone knew it was badly weakened by its flawed tires, and if Ford was going to open up yet another front against it, it could be the death knell.

So CEO Lampe and his team made a critical decision: counterattack.

Rather than wait for Ford to ask for another recall and then defend itself against the criticism, Firestone decided to preempt it. Firestone "fired" Ford, one of its largest customers, a move that would have been unthinkable just months earlier.

The battle was joined. Firestone hired experts, conducted tests, assembled data. They ran ads, hired lobbyists, retained a former high-level transportation department safety official, briefed reporters and courted consumer and safety advocates—all to bring attention to what Firestone believed were design flaws in the Explorer that made tire problems seem minor in comparison: the alleged propensity of the Explorer to roll over in an accident, especially when a tire blew out.

The effort reached its "high noon" moment in a pressure-packed hearing of the House Commerce Committee in which both corporations and their allies traded attacks, statistics, studies and accusations. But the line of the day came from Firestone's Lampe, who, testifying just minutes after Ford CEO Jacques Nasser, told the congressmen, "The loss of tread or the air in a tire shouldn't cause a driver to lose control of the vehicle; the driver should be able to pull over, not roll over."

Being able to hit from a defensive posture is hard for even the best boxers, but if you can master it, you can fight your way out of a lot of jams. We're not safety experts and we have no idea whether Firestone or Ford is right in this battle of the corporate behemoths. (In fact, Paul is the proud owner of not one but two Ford SUVs.) But as a matter of survival strategy, Lampe, Eller and their team at Firestone may have set a new standard for corporate disaster relief.

Okay, Okay, Let's Talk About Clinton

You already know how much we love Bill Clinton. It goes without saying, but we're going to say it anyway: We love the guy. He's been kind to our families, he's been more responsible for our success than anyone else and we believe he was a remarkably talented and successful president— perhaps the most intelligent president since Jefferson and the most politically talented since FDR.

And yet when he screwed up he didn't always handle it right.

We've come to terms with the fact that he didn't 'fess up. We still believe he would have been better off if he had. The advice he got—that the American people could not tolerate an adulterer in the White House and so he "just had to fight"—was wrong, wrong, wrong. The American people are not fragile, hothouse flowers. We're tough. We can take it. And with half of all marriages ending in divorce, chances are the Clinton family isn't the only one who's had to confront this problem.

But he didn't 'fess up. That violates our first rule for crisis management. That also made it impossible to set things right—until he finally, belatedly did 'fess up. (As for fighting back, we'll get to that in a minute.)

Where he excelled, however, was in keeping his eyes on the prize. He understood that his strength and his salvation would be from the American people, not the Beltway elites or the media, and certainly not from the laughingly named "independent counsel." And so he kept himself and his staff focused to the maximum extent possible on the serious business of running the country. When he told the American people that he got up every day and went to work to try to make their lives better, they believed him. Because it was true.

Obviously, it was morally wrong to have an affair and morally wrong to lie about it and cause others to lie for him. Those lies were also strategic mistakes that invited his adversaries to pounce on his lies when they realized the American people would forgive the affair. Still, the fact that Clinton beat back the impeachment lynch mob, saw Ken Starr leave his post a discredited man and finished his presidency as the most popular two-term president in the history of polling suggests that he had a pretty good overall strategy throughout the whole Lewinsky mess—a strategy that went far beyond his initial lies.

It is our view that Clinton's most serious strategic mistake (after refusing to come clean) was his now-infamous August 17, 1998, speech after his grand jury testimony. Paul was asked to draft a version of the speech even before Clinton had told him the truth. (He was able to make an educated guess as to the truth by reading the well-placed leaks in the paper every day.) Because he owes Clinton a debt of loyalty, Paul has never discussed that night or his private conversations with the president. He's not about to start now.

Suffice it to say, neither Paul nor James nor most of the people close to the president thought it was a good idea to attack Ken Starr in that speech. We take a backseat to no one in our disapproval of Starr and how he did his job. But as the Good Book says, there's a time and a place for everything, and the time to attack Starr was *not* at the moment Clinton was confessing to something he'd been falsely denying for eight months.

It was an enormous error and it threatened to rob Clinton of much of the goodwill he'd gained as the victim of the sex police. Orrin Hatch, a conservative Republican but not a hater by any means, was overheard after the speech muttering, "What a jerk." If the majority of the American people had felt that way, Clinton would have been through.

In fact, for a brief time an awful lot of Americans did feel that way. In the wake of that speech, Clinton's popularity dropped. It wasn't that people were shocked at the specter of infidelity. Rather, it was the whipsaw of seeing Clinton confess, apologize and attack all in one breath. Next time you've got to confess something and apologize for it, try adding, "And by the way, Herb down the street is a pig." Herb may well be a pig, but your wrongdoing is Topic A. Trying to shift the subject to someone else's faults looks like a cheap attempt to deflect attention—probably because it is.

Clinton was able to recover by making a second stab at The Apology—and then a third and a fourth and a fifth stab. With practice, he got real good at apologizing. His finest moment, though, was when he told a group of clergy gathered in the historic East Room of the White House, "There is no fancy way to say that I have sinned." In plain, unvarnished, unslick language he spoke about his failings, asked for forgiveness and even revealed that he was meeting with ministers on a regular basis to seek spiritual counsel through the ordeal.

That's the speech he should have given on August 17.

We all make mistakes. And yet we're always surprised—and unprepared to respond—when we do. Moreover, when you screw up you tend to doubt yourself all the more. You lose your self-confidence, your equilibrium. Folks tend to go into deep denial, which just insults the intelligence of everyone around you. Perhaps that's why it's so disarming and effective when people 'fess up and do what they can to set things right. This is one of those areas where the right thing to do is also the smart thing to do.

Sometimes There's Just No Way to Recover, So You Duck and Cover

The important lesson of this chapter is that you can recover from screwups if you keep your wits—and your ethics—about you.

But sometimes there's just no recovering—even if the screwup isn't yours. Case in point:

In the 1984 Doggett for Senate campaign in Texas, we knew they had a tough road ahead of them. It was the height of the Reagan Revolution, and Texas was the epicenter of Reagan Country. And then we heard about Tony Zule.

Tony Zule was a Doggett supporter in San Antonio. He approached Doggett at a fund-raiser and asked if he could have his picture taken presenting Doggett with a contribution. It happens every day in a campaign, and we thought nothing of it. Then the photo showed up in the San Antonio gay newspaper under the headline: LOCAL GAY FUNDRAISER BENEFITS DOGGETT.

It turns out that the check was the proceeds of—get this—a gay strip show. Featuring Frankie the Banana Queen and Mister Gay Apollo. The Republican candidate, Phil Gramm, caught wind of this (apparently old Phil had some friends who read the gay press; not that there's anything wrong with that) and pounced (figuratively speaking).

Gramm began blanketing the airwaves with a radio ad in which a motherly voice intoned, "I want to talk to you about family values and the United States Senate race here in Texas. Liberal Lloyd Doggett is raising money from all-male, nude, gay strip shows . . ." The redundancy of the language aside, the ad was hard to rebut. James called Tony Zule, who'd already boasted to the press that they'd even taken the tips from the strippers' G-strings and donated them to Doggett. (The first time we ever wished we'd received laundered money.)

We screamed and yelled and pointed out that we had nothing to do with the strip show. We said that Doggett didn't approve of fund-raisers at strip clubs, gay or straight. We pointed out that in a multimillion-dollar campaign the strip show had raised just $600. We complained that Gramm was gay-baiting.

Nothing worked.

Looking back, given the state and the time in which we were running, we would've lost anyway. Reagan destroyed Mondale, carrying Texas by 27.5 points. We only lost by 18 points.

The lesson? Sometimes you just gotta get your ass whipped. But over the long term, you can recover from that, too. We went on to have pretty good careers despite being wiped out in Texas in 1984. Doggett went on to serve on the Texas Supreme Court and is now the congressman from Austin and a respected member of the powerful House Ways & Means Committee.

Know What to Do When You Win

Now that you're nearly all the way through this book, and you've of course committed yourself to living by its precepts, be prepared to win. Forget all that crap we had at the beginning about how this book won't make you rich and successful and desirable. We had to put that in there to keep the lawyers off our butts. If you do the things we recommend in this book, you are sure to succeed.

Okay, maybe not always. But we do believe—in fact, we're convinced—that your chances to succeed are greater if you try some or all of these rules. So it wouldn't hurt to think a little about what you're going to do with your soon-to-be success.

It seems like a high-class problem, what to do once you've won. But in reality more people than you would think sow the seeds of their own destruction just as they're achieving victory.

First because no victory is ever final. Okay, so the battle

of Nagasaki was pretty final. But short of an unconditional surrender forced by atomic weaponry, no victory is ever final.

The *Splat* Ceremony

One of the most entertaining and beloved pastimes of modern America is the *Splat* Ceremony. You know it well: A hero is discovered, lauded, puffed up and placed on a pedestal. The higher the pedestal, the better. The poor schmuck thinks this high pedestal befits his great talent and extraordinary achievements.

Is he ever wrong.

The reason some folks put other folks so high on a pedestal is because they love to hear the *SPLAT!* when they hit the ground.

Or as retired General Norman Schwarzkopf says, "The higher up a monkey climbs, the easier it is to see its ass."

Every child on every playing field learns this lesson: The bigger they are, the harder they fall. They learn that cliché for a reason. Because it's true. The challenge is to get big and not fall. That takes some skill, some grace and some luck.

James had a classic Washington wake-up call after Bill Clinton was elected president. He and his wife were invited to a dinner party to celebrate the birthday of Al Hunt of *The Wall Street Journal*. James was feeling quite pleased with himself as he got ready to go to the party; Al Hunt was (and is) one of the classiest, smartest and most decent people in Washington. His wife, Judy Woodruff, is a star anchor for CNN and their friends are definitely A-list. James smugly felt as if he'd arrived.

At the end of the dinner Sally Quinn, the unofficial permanent queen of social Washington, turned to James, quite matter-of-factly, and said, "It's going to be interesting. I hope you make it." The implication was clear: Lots of hot new cowboys ride into this town, only to be thrown in the dirt. Maybe James could handle Washington; maybe Washington would handle James. And Miss Sally wasn't placing any bets either way.

Paul had a similar experience a year earlier. When Harris Wofford was elected to the United States Senate from Pennsylvania in 1991, it was the biggest thing to hit the political world in years. Wofford was a relatively unknown candidate (although he had been an aide to Martin Luther King Jr. and John F. Kennedy). He defeated the former governor and then–Bush administration's attorney general, Richard Thornburgh.

Wofford began the campaign 47 points behind, yet rallied to win by 10 points, producing that rarest of political gems: an upset landslide. Some people win in an upset, but it's usually close. Others win in a runaway, but it's usually evident weeks before the election. In Wofford's case he never led in a published poll, but the trajectory of his ascent and the power of his message ("If a criminal has the right to see a lawyer, why don't working people have the right to see a doctor?") allowed him to slingshot past Thornburgh at the end.

The Republicans didn't know what hit them. The Democrats saw (correctly, it turned out) a harbinger of victory against Bush in the upcoming 1992 presidential election. The political press loved the story—David versus Goliath, the tweedy, professorial intellectual defeats the popular, successful politician. And since Paul had been Wofford's campaign manager, he was suddenly thrust into the spotlight.

JAMES CARVILLE & PAUL BEGALA

When the *McNeil-Lehrer NewsHour* asked Paul to appear, he was sure he'd made it. At the age of thirty he was entering the big time, about to go on national television to explain to the world just how brilliant he was.

Before the interview, Paul received a call from Mark Shields, the brilliant commentator and columnist who'd been a successful political strategist before moving into the top ranks of the punditocracy. Shields had known Paul for years and had promoted his career relentlessly, undeterred by Paul's early series of flops. Now Shields was offering advice like a Dutch uncle.

"You are about to have a terrible thing happen to you," he said. "You're about to know success at a young age." He warned Paul not to believe his own B.S., told him that humility is a lot more attractive than arrogance and lectured that he did not win the race; the candidate did. Paul took Shields's advice, and it probably saved him from making a complete ass of himself the first time he went on national TV. (Shields, it should be noted, cannot be held responsible for the many times Paul has subsequently made an ass of himself on national TV.)

Deny the Credit for Winning, Take Responsibility for Losing

We're not into false modesty; some of our campaigns featured lame candidates who won on the strength of our strategy. But the big wins of our career were much more a function of the candidate than the strategists. True aficionados understood that.

We touched on this in Rule Eleven (on recovering from screwups), but let us state it more bluntly: Taking responsibility makes it less likely that you'll actually be saddled with it; the converse is true of credit. If you deny credit, it's more likely to come to you. Had we run around the country trying to tell people we were the genuises who got Bill Clinton elected, human nature would have kept folks from actually giving us the credit.

Finally, taking credit for yourself has a demoralizing effect on your team. Unless you're a runner or a poker player, chances are whatever success you may enjoy truly is the result of a team effort.

Remember: Once you've won, the goal is not to gloat; it's to win another one. Do everything you can to set yourself up for another victory. Do nothing that will make your next effort more difficult.

Never Fight a Battle You're Not Prepared to Win

This is an important concept in military strategy; it ought to be important to your strategy. That's not to say never fight a battle you're not *likely* to win. That's a different matter altogether. Sometimes you've got to fight even when you know the odds are long—or even hopeless. Masada and the Alamo come to mind.

Everyone says, "Pick your battles," and they're right. But usually they only mean "Pick your battles based on whether or not you have a good chance to win." That's fine, as far as it goes. But we think you should be even pickier. Only pick battles that are: a) winnable; b) important; c) battles for which you're fully prepared to pay the price to win; and d) battles that you're damn sure you can afford to win.

The notion of a Pyrrhic victory—a win at too high a price—comes from military lore. Pyrrhus was a king of Epirus who lived in the third century B.C. In 279 B.C. he decided to take on the mighty Roman army. But before he sailed for Italy, Cineas, his chief ambassador, had the following conversation with him (which was faithfully recorded by the great ancient historian Plutarch).

Cineas began: "The Romans are reported to be great warriors and conquerors of many nations. If the gods permit us to overcome them, how shall we use our victory?"

"That is an easy question," responded Pyrrhus. "Once we conquer the Romans, there will not be any city in all of Italy that will resist us."

Cineas paused, then asked: "Once we have Italy, what next?"

"Sicily, which is a wealthy island, should be easy to take," said Pyrrhus.

Cineas continued: "You speak what is perfectly probable, but will the possession of Sicily put an end to the war?"

"Carthage and Africa would then be within reach," said Pyrrhus, "and once we have them, who in the world would dare to oppose us?"

"No one, certainly," said Cineas, "And then what shall we do?"

Pyrrhus still did not see where he had been led by this argument, so he said: "Then, my dear Cineas, we will relax, and drink all day, and amuse ourselves with pleasant conversation."

"What prevents us from doing that now?" said Cineas. "We already have enough to make that possible without any more hard work, suffering, and danger."

But Pyrrhus didn't get the point. He attacked and defeated the Roman army at Asculum in Apulia. He won, but his casualties were so heavy that he wryly observed, "One more such victory and I am lost." Indeed, later his weakened army attacked Sparta and lost. Pyrrhus was hunted down and killed by an angry mob in the streets of Argos. Now you know why Plutarch dubbed Pyrrhus "the Fool of Hope."[1]

The Gus Factor

In less classical terms, we call it the Gus Factor. When he was a teenager, Paul had a dog named Gus. Ol' Gus was a great dog, but he had one flaw: He liked to chase cars. Paul tried everything to break him of this habit to no avail. And like all owners of car-chasing dogs, Paul occasionally joked about what Gus might do when he finally caught one.

Then one day he did.

Or, rather, the car caught him. It was one of those monster Buicks of the late '70s, and it sent ol' Gus to the Great Car Chase in the Sky.

While they didn't call it that, the Gus Factor played an important role in the first Bush administration's decision not to topple Saddam Hussein when they had him by the short-and-curlies at the end of the Persian Gulf War. Bush senior and his national security team were prepared for a partial victory—driving Iraqi troops out of Kuwait, restoring the Al-Sabbah monarchy to power, protecting oil-drunk Saudi Arabia. But they were unwilling to pay the price of total victory. They feared that removing Saddam from power might result in someone worse replacing him (one of the great, unprovable arguments that establishment types love; the truth is, the replacement is almost never as bad as the predecessor. When Slobodan Milosevic was driven from power, he was replaced by a much better guy. And it's kind of hard to imagine someone worse than Saddam—who used chemical weapons on his own people).

The Bushies were also unwilling to pay the price of occupation and "nation building," the strategy that worked so well in Japan and Germany after World War II, but it would have been expensive, demanding, lengthy and unpopular in the 1990s. Finally, they feared the chaos from a potential breakup of Iraq into three or more separate entities, which would end Iraq's occasionally useful role as a counterbalance to Iran. So, applying the Gus Factor, Bush senior decided he didn't want to chase that car. (In point of fact, your authors are split on this one; one of us agrees with Bush, one of us doesn't. We'll leave it to you to guess which one.)

The Gus Factor is also useful when pondering your next career move. When Bill Bradley announced that he would not run for reelection to the Senate in 1996, John F. Kennedy Jr. was approached about running. He thought about it. Public service was obviously in his blood, but not in his immediate plans. He'd launched *George* magazine not long before and had a dream of making politics relevant and interesting again. But opportunity knocked. What to do? Paul was working with John on *George* at the time and he applied the Gus Factor. "What if you win? Then where will you be?" he asked John. With an ironic laugh, John admitted that he hadn't considered that. He'd thought about the race and the magazine and the impact on his life, but he hadn't really thought through the full consequences of winning. Did he really want to be a United States senator from New Jersey? He took a pass; the timing was wrong. But if it hadn't been for the tragedy that struck on that foggy summer night, we're convinced that John would have one day applied the Gus test and come to a very different conclusion.

The same principle applies in business. It may sound great if you land a sale fifty times larger than anything your company has ever handled before. But if you do that with-out the rest of the team behind you, manufacturing is going to tell you they can't deliver that kind of quantity on time with guaranteed quality; labor is going to tell you they want time and a half for overtime and double pay for weekends; legal is going to tell you the company's going to get its ass sued. And instead of being the hero, you're going to be a fool.

Touch a King, Kill a King

This is just another way of saying, "In for a penny, in for a pound." If you're going for a promotion or for a big sale, or if you're going after someone who's your rival, make sure it's a fight you want. Don't do it half-assed.

Be prepared to pay the price. If you get your way—especially if it requires rolling over someone—you may win. But the price of winning is that all the friends and the allies and the teammates of the person you've beaten are going to be your enemies for a long, long time. They'll re-sent you. They'll be angry with you. They'll try to under-mine you. They'll lay traps for you.

So don't only think of the price of defeat. Think of the price of victory.

Sometimes it's a price worth paying. Lord knows every-one who loves Ken Starr (both of them) and everyone who loves George W. Bush can't stand us. We went after those guys publicly, with everything we had. We used facts, argu-mentation, research, humor, ridicule and (in James's case) some damn good recipes. Now we have a rather large col-lection of people who can't stand us. That's a price we were willing to pay.

Franklin Roosevelt understood that there were advantages to having the right enemies. He called those who opposed his liberal economic policies "economic royalists" and said of them, "They are unanimous in their hatred of me—and I welcome their hatred." That wasn't just rhetoric for FDR (although it was pretty good rhetoric). It was a statement of his strategy. Roosevelt knew that his New Deal program was just as unpopular with the moneyed elite as it was popular among ordinary citizens. So he welcomed the fact that his policies made him a marked man among some—as long as that "some" wasn't more than half the electorate. FDR didn't win four presidential elections by being a bad politician. The folks who opposed the New Deal—the people FDR derided as "economic royalists"— went after FDR. But instead of killing him, their attacks only made him stronger. And FDR knew that his New Deal was well worth incurring the eternal wrath of the moneyed elite.

Don't Sweat the Small Stuff

If the battle is important enough, if it's winnable and you're prepared to pay the price of long-lasting bitterness from those you've defeated, go for it. If not, don't go into battle. Compromise—or beat a tactical retreat (see Rule Five). How do you know when to fight and when to let it pass? It takes experience and good judgment (which, it has been said, is born of bad experiences and poor judgment).

President Clinton was a great one for preaching that there are few final victories in life. When he put us in charge of the War Room, rather than seeing it as a victory over our rivals within the campaign, he gave us a firm order: "Don't rub anyone's nose in it." More than any other politician we've ever known, Clinton understands that today's adversary may be tomorrow's ally. He loves to quote Abraham Lincoln: "I destroy my enemies. I make them my friends."

Back during the worst of the congressional investigations into Whitewater, in July 1996, TWA Flight 800 crashed off the coast of New York's Long Island. Clinton ordered up Air Force One and instructed his staff to invite New York's two senators to fly with him to the state to comfort the families of the victims and see what could be done to aid the relief effort and the investigation. Clinton didn't care that one of the senators was Alphonse D'Amato, the Republican chairman of the Senate Banking Committee who was at that time the president's chief persecutor on Whitewater. Clinton believed that no purpose would have been served in excluding one of New York's senators from a mission of mercy just because he was leading a bogus investigation.

Clinton looked magnanimous, D'Amato was doubtless grateful, and D'Amato's advisers would later come to the conclusion that his foray into investigating the president had hurt the senator politically. Indeed, D'Amato later opposed further congressional digging into Whitewater.[2]

This was the same thinking that led Clinton to name Mike McCurry as his State Department spokesman and later White House press secretary. You doubtless remember McCurry as the witty, unflappable presence at the White House podium, protecting Clinton from the jackals of the press corps. But hard-line Clinton loyalists after the 1992 election saw McCurry as the enemy. He had worked for Bob Kerrey, one of Clinton's opponents in the Democratic primaries, and Kerrey's operation was widely believed to have spread some especially nasty stories about Clinton's personal life.

Clinton could not have cared less. He reasoned that he

had nothing to lose and everything to gain by bringing Mc-Curry on board. Overlooking McCurry's recent past was a classy move and a smart one. McCurry became one of Clinton's most valuable staff members, and Clinton got one of the most talented spin doctors in America on his team. It was this sort of reasoning that led Lyndon Johnson, in a similar situation, to say of a former adversary he hired, "I'd rather have him inside the tent pissing out than outside pissing in."

Letting the small differences slide is especially important with someone who is already a part of your organization. There's always someone in every campaign who has his or her own agenda. It's often a perfectly noble one—maybe he's a big supporter of historic preservation. As a campaign manager you can't let your candidate spend a lot of time on an issue that's at best esoteric, and extraneous to the message to boot. But if the historic-preservation fanatic is one of your best staffers, do you really want to kill his one dream?

So you let the candidate do a 9 P.M. drop-by at a gathering of historic preservationists. You tell the travel aide to get the candidate the hell out of there after thirty minutes, and everybody's happy. As campaign manager you could have just ground the historic-preservation guy's nose in it. But it's the better part of valor to keep him happy and productive, so you don't sweat the small stuff.

Be Gracious in Victory

Okay, we admit it. This is not our long suit. We come from a world in which victory is everything. But elections are just one part of politics. After an election there's usually a long, long road. So although it may be as difficult for you as it is for us, it's important to be a good winner.

After both the Wofford victory in 1991 and the Clinton win in 1992, Paul told reporters: "The candidate was Secretariat. I was Ron Turcotte." Turcotte was a great jockey, but the reporters who cover horse racing must be smarter than political reporters, because they never give undue credit to the jockey. They recognized that Secretariat was a once-in-a-lifetime horse. At other times Paul would say, "I know the difference between the organ grinder and the monkey."

Those sayings have the added benefit, as Henry Kissinger once observed in another context, of being true.

When the Republican-controlled Senate overwhelmingly acquitted President Clinton at the end of the impeachment trial, Clinton had every right to gloat. His popularity was near an all-time high; the American people overwhelmingly viewed the impeachment as unfair, unwise, unjust, unwarranted and unconstitutional. Clinton not only received "Not guilty" votes from every Democrat in the Senate, he was also found innocent by enough Republicans to deny the House "managers" even a majority (the Constitution requires a two-thirds supermajority to convict and remove a president).

We believe that the trial, and the acquittal, vindicated Clinton in the eyes of history. But instead of gloating, instead of high-fiving, instead of attacking (as he did so disastrously in the speech after his grand jury testimony), Clinton was humble in victory. As Paul worked on the speech for him, Clinton stressed that he wanted to convey to the country how sorry he was for what we'd gone through and to open the door to begin the healing.

Alone, he strode to a podium in the Rose Garden and delivered a speech that lasted less than a minute and a half. This is all he said:

Now that the Senate has fulfilled its constitutional responsibility, bringing this process to a conclusion, I want to say again to the American people how profoundly sorry I am for what I said and did to trigger these events and the great burden they have imposed on the Congress and on the American people.

I also am humbled and very grateful for the support and the prayers I have received from millions of Americans over this past year.

Now I ask all Americans, and I hope all Americans, here in Washington and throughout our land, will rededicate ourselves to the work of serving our nation and building our future together.

This can be and this must be a time of reconciliation and renewal for America.

Thank you very much.

He didn't even mention that he'd won. He sought no vindication, nor did he claim victory. Rather, he humbly apologized for what he'd done wrong, asked all Americans to reunite. He put exactly the right tone on his painful, costly, divisive victory. That graciousness helped him maintain the support of the American people, and perhaps even the grudging respect of his Republican adversaries, which he would need as he went on to lead America to victory in the Kosovo conflict.

Part of being a gracious winner is allowing your opponent to save face. That's not always possible, and it certainly isn't possible in an election (barring a withdrawal, which isn't much of a face-saving move). Ulysses S. Grant was a brilliant general; in many ways he was the first man to fully understand the import of modern, industrialized warfare. But his insistence on unconditional surrender brought a heavy price. The South, long on pride and short on industrial output, was systematically incapacitated. And General Sherman's pyrotechnic travels didn't help much either. To this day there are still folks in our beloved South filled with bitter resentment over the War of Northern Aggression.

Lincoln understood the awful price of unconditional surrender. Not long before he was killed, he was being serenaded on the grounds of the White House by cheering bands of supporters who were celebrating the Union's victory. Lincoln came to the White House window to receive the adulation of the crowd. When they asked their victorious president what song he'd like to hear to mark the moment, he stunned the crowd by saying "Dixie."

One of history's greatest "what-ifs" is what would have happened to Reconstruction if Lincoln had not been murdered. If his famous maxim, "With malice toward none, with charity toward all," had really been the guiding principle of Reconstruction, would the South have remained so bitter for so long? Perhaps. The legacy of slavery is a bitter one. But as southerners we believe that Lincoln was the greatest American who ever lived, in part because of his commitment to healing. And the nation would have healed much faster under his leadership.

This is not an absolute rule. Unconditional surrender was the only moral course when the civilized world confronted Hitler. One of the great humanitarians of history, Albert Einstein, was the one who first urged FDR to develop an atomic bomb. He knew that Hitler was working on one, and he understood the truly evil nature of Nazism. Given that reality, the only acceptable outcome for World War II was not merely victory, but total victory. The complete dismantling of the Third Reich, the trial, conviction and execution of the monsters who masterminded the Final Solution, years of occupation, division and the long, slow rebirth of German democracy.

And yet historians agree that the savage terms of the Treaty of Versailles that ended World War I played a large role in creating the climate of resentment and hatred that made Hitler's rise possible.

How do you know the difference between World War I and World War II? It's hard. The best we can say is if you come to the conclusion that you're facing someone who is implacably and permanently opposed to you, your friends, your company, your cause and everything you stand for, then you're in one of those rare situations in which you have to fight until you've received an unconditional surrender.

So it was in the people versus Ken Starr. The Clinton-Starr struggle was a mano-a-mano clash in which one man would be left standing and one man would not. We have no regrets for any of the things we said about Starr, and nothing but pride for the battle we waged against him.

Not every battle allows the option of giving your opponent a graceful exit. But when that possibility exists, you won't regret taking it.

Consolidate Your Gains

Don't get so carried away with being gracious in victory that you forget what you were fighting for. Remember what the slave was ordered to repeat to Caesar as the emperor rode triumphantly through Rome: "Sic transit gloria mundi"—all glory of this world is fleeting.

All victories are fleeting, too. So when you win one, move quickly and decisively to consolidate your gains. First because it will show that you're not like a dog that's caught a car—you actually know what you want to do with the prize once you've won it. Also because consolidating your gains will make it more difficult for a successor or a rival to undo what you've done.

Lyndon Johnson wasn't the smoothest or the handsomest president we ever had. But he damn sure knew how to consolidate his gains. He ascended to the presidency in tragedy, but he immediately set out to consolidate his gains, knowing full well that the chance to make his mark was fleeting. On the first full day of his presidency, between receiving foreign dignitaries and trying to calm a nation staggering with grief, Johnson told the chairman of the Council of Economic Advisers to go to work crafting a war on poverty. "Give it the highest priority," Johnson said. "Push ahead full-tilt."

Perhaps sensing that the country was in a precarious position, perhaps knowing that the combination of a looming land war in Asia and domestic strife at home could swamp his presidency, Johnson moved "full-tilt" to consolidate his power and enact as much of his progressive agenda as he could. Medicare, Medicaid, Head Start, the Voting Rights Act, the Civil Rights Act, fair housing laws and more. Since LBJ's presidency the White House has bounced back and forth between Republicans and Democrats five times. But none of those presidents have succeeded in repealing the core of Johnson's Great Society.

That's what we call knowing how to consolidate your gains.

Take Even More Risks

Most politicians, most businesspeople, most folks of any kind, become more risk-averse as they grow older—and especially if they've enjoyed a measure of success. Earlier in their career it's easier to take a big risk because there's time to recover from a big failure. But then something happens. Something that is at once both completely understandable and completely illogical. Risk taking breeds success. Success breeds risk aversion. And risk aversion breeds stagnation and failure. It is so much harder to keep taking risks after you've enjoyed success. But it's the only way to continue to succeed.

Take Jack Welch, for example. As he neared the end of his remarkable, twenty-year run at the helm of GE, Welch was universally acclaimed as the greatest CEO of postwar American history. He'd taken GE from being a sleepy light-bulb company to being the most successful corporation in the world, or so the legend said.

In 2000, Welch was busy planning his retirement and a smooth transfer to his successor. Ninety-nine percent of other business leaders would never have dreamed of trying anything riskier than a long five-iron shot over a bunker onto the green. But Welch decided he had one last big, bold gamble in him. He launched a multibillion-dollar merger with the electronics firm Honeywell.

After a long fight with European Union regulators, the deal went bust. The critics were, predictably, merciless: Welch had tarnished his image. He had set about a high-risk strategy that, even if the deal had gone through, would have saddled his successor with even greater transition problems. He had lost his touch, was trying desperately to reclaim his faded magic.

Baloney.

Welch got to the top by taking risks, and we love the fact that as long as he was in the game, he *played* the game. So what if one deal or another falls through? The important thing is that, over time, the vast majority of Welch's bold risks paid off. You can afford a lot of Honeywell debacles if you've got a twenty-year track record of sustained success.

Oh, and by the way, even with the Honeywell deal going kaput, GE reported a 15 percent jump in its profit as this book was going to press.[3]

A more famous—and more successful—example of a legend who kept taking risks after he'd already had it made is Ted Williams of the Boston Red Sox. In 1941 Williams was vying to break the magic mark of batting .400 in a season. On the second-to-the-last day of the season, Williams went one for four, which reduced his average from .4009 to .39955. Because baseball's rules would have rounded William's average up to .400, Red Sox manager Joe Cronin offered to bench Williams for the season-ending double-header in Philadelphia's Shibe Park—thus preserving one of the most difficult feats in sports.

Sitting out was the only logical thing to do. Williams's Boston Red Sox were out of contention for the pennant already, so the team didn't need him or the wins. And Williams's batting average was perched so precariously on the bubble of .400 that the odds were good that he'd fall below .400. All it would take was a couple of unlucky breaks—a bad call on a third strike or a lucky play in the field—and everything that Williams had worked so hard for all season would be lost.

Nobody would have blamed the Splendid Splinter if he had gathered a few splinters in his rear riding the pine to protect his precious and rare gem of a batting average. In short, Williams had everything to lose and nothing to gain by playing.

Williams played. "Not play? Christ, I was going to play. I never even gave anything else a thought."[4]

Years later, Williams's former teammate and childhood friend Bobby Doerr said: "To tell you the truth, I'm surprised old blue-eyed Ted didn't punch Joe for suggesting it."[5]

Williams attacked the ball with a vengeance. In the opening game of the twin bill he went four for five—hitting three singles and his thirty-seventh home run of the year and leading his team to a 12–11 victory over the Athletics.

Williams's average was now well above .400 with no rounding. Think about it. What would you do? All you have to do to achieve one of your fondest goals in life is to sit down.

But they didn't call Williams "Teddy Ballgame" for nothing. He didn't think twice about coming out of the lineup for the final game. He doubled and singled in that second game, going two for three before the game was called because of darkness after seven innings.

After his six-for-eight day, Ted Williams had a final average of .4057, which was rounded up to an astonishing .406. The following morning the Boston papers quoted Williams as saying, "I gave it a good day."[6]

Fifty years later Teddy Ballgame told the Bergen *Record:* "I would have been the most disappointed guy in the world if I didn't make it."

In the sixty years since Williams's amazing, gutsy season, no one has hit .400.

One of the things we like about sports and politics is that, at the end of the day, they tote up the scores and publicly brand you a winner or a loser. In a more subtle way, every business is like that. Big businesses have quarterly statements and annual reports, Securities and Exchange Commission filings and proxy statements. And small-business people have the terror of the bottom line and the expectant looks of employees who'd like to be paid every week.

Show business has its own merciless accountability, too: the all-powerful box office. Even the most bankable stars are, in the words of the cruel but true Hollywood axiom, "only as good as their last picture." The seemingly random nature of success in the entertainment community, combined with the very public humiliation of failing, make for some very risk-averse people. And who can blame them? If you've had a big hit with, say, *Porky's,* why not make *Porky's II: The Next Day,* then *Porky's Revenge,* and on and on.

That's why we especially admire creative people who continue to take risks once they've succeeded, people who refuse to stay in the rut, who experiment and dare greatly—and sometimes fail greatly.

One of our favorites is Steven Spielberg. His first feature film was *The Sugarland Express,* which he filmed in Sugar Land, Texas. Paul was a kid in school in Sugar Land at the time, and he remembers the movie as the biggest thing to hit town during his childhood. *The Sugarland Express* was a good flick; a prison-break film with a twist (it's worth renting if you want a slice of small-town Texas life in the early 1970s, as well as one of Goldie Hawn's best early performances), but it didn't exactly rock the box offices.

Undeterred, Spielberg set out to make a film of the best-selling Peter Benchley novel *Jaws.* Filming the movie was a logistical nightmare, with underwater scenes, shark attacks and even a shark exploding (we don't want to ruin the film for you if you've never seen it). Spielberg's perseverance and creativity paid off. *Jaws* became the top-grossing film of all time (until it was surpassed by other Spielberg blockbusters).

From there Spielberg had a parade of successes: *Close Encounters of the Third Kind, Raiders of the Lost Ark, Poltergeist, E.T.* and *Jurassic Park.* Each movie grossed millions, and Spielberg was the king of Hollywood. He could have produced Cineplex smash after Cineplex smash, made millions (really, a billion or two) and been content with being the most successful and respected person in show business.

But just when he had it made, Spielberg took the biggest risk of his professional life. He decided to make a movie about the Holocaust. The greatest evil in human history is not exactly the kind of topic that packs 'em in at mall theaters. And how do you convey a horror so vast? This was not a job for mechanical sharks, special-effect demons or high-tech dinosaurs. The villain here was real. It was evil incarnate.

Spielberg selected the novel *Schindler's List,* which was based on the true story of a Polish businessman who used Jews for free labor but who ultimately used the ruse of employment to save 1,100 Jews from the Holocaust. Sensitive to criticism that Auschwitz itself should not be used as a movie set, Spielberg built a replica outside the walls of the real death camp. The film, shot in black and white, is heartbreaking, tragic and life-changing. To watch it is to be torn up inside, and when you put yourself back together again, you're never quite the same. Many believe it to be a modern classic.

But not everyone.

Conservative Republican congressman Tom Coburn of Oklahoma attacked Spielberg and his film when it was shown on television. "I cringe when I realize that there were children all across this nation watching this program," he said. "They were exposed to the violence of multiple-gunshot head wounds, vile language, full-frontal nudity and irresponsible sexual activity." Coburn threatened to punish TV networks with legislation mandating stricter ratings.

Spielberg got it just as bad from the left. A leftist professor wrote that Spielberg's film "deliberately ignores the historical context of the Shoah. Worse, if people follow the prompting of the film, they will re-create the conditions that made fascism possible.

"Schindler's List avoids any mention of the anti-fascist resistance and the centripetal role communists played in its leadership," he continued. "Within the vacuum of resistance, the film offers an anti-Semitic vision of Jews. The only developed Jewish characters are swindlers, collaborators, connivers: stereotypes. Working-class Jews, as in all of anti-Semitism, are fleeting vapors. In fact, the Soviet Red Army, which played the decisive role in both resistance to the Holocaust and in all of WWII, liberated the 'Schindler Jews.' "[7]

The right thought Spielberg was corrupting the morals of our children. The left accused him of anti-Semitism. You wonder if Spielberg ever thought he should have been content filming chase scenes between Harrison Ford and make-believe Nazis as they pursued a mythical archaeological treasure.

We hope, however, that Spielberg feels the rare satisfaction of someone who took risks he didn't have to take but somehow needed to. Of course, it's nice that the risk paid off—with Academy Awards and international praise, which more than answered the attackers. But that's really beside the point. The highest praise we can give him is that he has pulled off the rarest win of all. The victory of someone who risked it all when he already had everything to lose.

The best thing to do when you've won is set yourself up for your next win. Be gracious and generous (for prudent reasons if not altruistic ones). And most of all, keep swinging.

The notion of resting on your laurels is a stupid one. Okay, when you retire, it's fine. But even then you're going to need some kind of challenge to keep you going. Resting on your laurels is overrated. All that happens is that your ass gets fat and your laurels get flat.

Paul Begala's Boys' French Toast

One of the things you do when you win is celebrate. The Carville-Matalin girls love to celebrate on Sunday morning by eating Daddy's French Toast. When the Begala boys came to visit for the weekend, they fell in love with "Uncle James's" French Toast and lavishly praised it (see, even kids can benefit from sucking up).

The Carville-Matalin girls have commemorated this celebration by renaming Daddy's French Toast "Paul Begala's Boys' French Toast." Here's the recipe that has the next generation swooning.

1 large egg
2 tbsp. unsalted butter, melted, plus extra for frying
¾ cup milk
2 tsp. vanilla extract
2 tbsp. sugar

⅓ cup all-purpose flour
¼ tsp. salt
4 to 5 slices day-old challah, ¾-inch thick (or 6 to 8 slices day-old sandwich bread)

Heat a 10- to 12-inch skillet (preferably a cast-iron one) over medium heat for 5 minutes. Meanwhile, beat the egg lightly in a shallow pan or pie plate; whisk in the butter, then the milk and vanilla, and finally the sugar, flour, and salt, continuing to whisk until smooth.

Soak a bread slice without oversaturating, about 40 seconds per side for challah (30 seconds per side for sandwich bread). Pick up the bread and allow the excess batter to drip off; repeat with remaining slices.

Swirl 1 tablespoon butter in the hot skillet. Transfer the prepared bread to the skillet; cook until golden brown, about 1 minute, 45 seconds on first side and 1 minute on the second.

Serve immediately. Continue, adding 1 tablespoon butter to the skillet for each new batch.

From: *The Cook's Bible*

Conclusion

WE don't know if you've learned anything from reading this book, but we sure learned a lot from writing it.

We learned that if you've been doing something all your life, something that's become second nature to you, it's useful to step back and reexamine it. First, principles and basic assumptions need to be analyzed from time to time, and that's what this book did for us. One of the important lessons we learned is that while Madison was right that men are not angels (nor are most women), the supposed tension between doing the right thing and doing the efficacious thing is overblown.

Being decent and gracious and honest, sharing credit and taking responsibility, recognizing the hidden strengths in others, fighting on no matter what, these are eternal verities. They are also very often highly effective strategies for success. In our own lives and careers, we must admit, we've often honored those rules of decency in the breach. But now that we've preached those virtues we're doubly committed to actually trying to practice them.

That's not to say that there's still no place for smash-mouth, in-your-face, rock 'em, sock 'em, gut-punching, heart-wrenching politics. We love a good fight as much as the next person—or, actually, more than any other people we know. So don't think we've gone soft. After decades in the political arena we're still proud to be combatants, gladiators in the greatest game we've ever seen. We still think Democrats are right and Republicans are wrong. But that's another book.

Finally, we were surprised as we wrote this book at how, well, *obvious* some of the rules are. Our seventh-grade football coaches taught us to work hard and never quit—and they were seventh-grade football coaches, not former presidential advisers. Still, there's great wisdom in the most basic of rules. Our goal in this book was to present rules that actually work in the real world, no matter how simple on the one hand or counterintuitive on the other. (How many other self-help books actively and directly advocate kissing ass?)

Nearly every lesson, example and anecdote in this book comes from a politician—most of whom we worked for. So we leave this project once again thanking the many men and women who took a chance on hiring us, who stuck with us when we had outrageous ideas, who stood by us when we were controversial and who paid us for doing a job we loved.

Source Notes

- **RULE ONE: DON'T QUIT. DON'T EVER QUIT.**
  1. http://yankees.mlb.com/NASApp/mlb/nyy/history/nyy_ history_timeline.jsp?period=5
  2. http://showcase.netins.net/web/creative/lincoln/speeches/ failures.htm
  3. National Parks Service list of Civil War battlefields and the results of those battles, http://www2.cr.nps.gov/abpp/ battles/bycampgn.htm
  4. Casey autobiography, quoted in the *Pittsburgh Post-Gazette,* May 31, 2000
  5. T. Roosevelt, "Citizenship in a Republic," speech at the Sorbonne, April 23, 1910, *Respectfully Quoted,* page 4

- **RULE TWO: KISS ASS**
  1. http://www.yendor.com/vanished/falklands-war.html
  2. http://www.spartacus.schoolnet.co.uk/PRchamberlain. htm
  3. http://library.byu.edu/~rdh/eurodocs/uk/peace.html

- **RULE THREE: KICK ASS**
  1. http://www.expage.com/boxing530
  2. *USA Today,* February 20, 1992
  3. *The Hutchinson Family Encyclopedia,* www.whsmithon-

line.co.uk/htmldata/encycasp?mainpage=http://books.wh
smithonline.co.uk/encyclopedia/so/Q0008450.htm
4. www.geocities.com/pattonhq/textfiles/thirdhst.html
5. www.brainyquote.com/quotes/quotes/j/q109216.html
6. www.closecombat.org/quotes.html

• RULE FOUR: FRAME THE DEBATE
1. *Meet the Press,* February 8, 1998

• RULE SEVEN: KNOW HOW TO COMMUNICATE
1. Bill Niekirk, *Chicago Tribune,* September 1, 1985
2. Posner, *Citizen Perot,* p. 66
3. Germond & Witcover, *Mad as Hell: Revolt at the Ballot Box, 1992,* pp. 488–89

• RULE EIGHT: WORK YOUR ASS OFF
1. *The Washington Post,* December 6, 1994
2. *The Hill,* May 19, 1999
3. *Texas Monthly,* September 1996
4. *The New York Times,* October 22, 2000
5. *Rochester Democrat and Chronicle,* October 28, 2000
6. *Albany Times-Union,* October 29, 2000

• RULE NINE: TURN WEAKNESS INTO STRENGTH
1. Posner, *Citizen Perot,* pp. 29, 44
2. *Fast Company,* April 1996

• RULE TEN: BE NIMBLE, JACK
1. *The Wall Street Journal,* October 26, 1994
2. http://www.americanpresident.org/KoTrain/Courses/RN/RN_Foreign_Affairs.htm
3. http://www.americanpresident.org/KoTrain/Courses/RN/RN_In_Brief.htm
4. Wallace timeline from www.pbs.org/wgbh/amex/wallace/timeline/index_3.html. Wallace quotes from www.pbs.org/wgbh/amex/wallace/sfeature/quotes.html

● **RULE TWELVE: KNOW WHAT TO DO WHEN YOU WIN**
1. www.e-classics.com/pyrrhus.htm
2. *The New York Times,* November 8, 1996. http://archive.nandotimes.com/nt/Elex96/11.7.96/1108inquiry.html
3. *The Wall Street Journal,* July 13, 2001
4. "1941: The Summer of .406," Tracy Ringolsby, *Seattle Times,* April 14, 1991
5. "Ted Williams' Quest to Be the Best," Bill Pennington, *The Record,* August 11, 1991
6. Ibid.
7. Rich Gibson, associate professor of Social Studies in the College of Education at San Diego State University. http://www-rohan.sdsu.edu/~rgibson/SchindlerListCrit2001.htm

About the Authors

JAMES CARVILLE has managed more political campaigns than anyone in history. He is the author of five books: *All's Fair* (with Mary Matalin); *We're Right, They're Wrong;* . . . *And the Horse He Rode in On; Stickin': The Case for Loyalty* and *Had Enough?* He lives in Virginia with his wife and two daughters.

PAUL BEGALA has served as Counselor to the President in the Clinton White House. He was a senior strategist to the 1992 Clinton-Gore campaign and has run political campaigns in the United States and abroad. He is a noted political commentator and Research Professor of Public Policy and Government at Georgetown University. The author of *"Is Our Children Learning?": The Case Against George W. Bush* and *It's Still the Economy, Stupid,* Begala lives in Virginia with his wife and four sons.